Desegregating
America's
Colleges

William M. Boyd, II
foreword by Clark Kerr

Published in cooperation with
The Educational Policy Center, Inc.

The Praeger Special Studies program—utilizing the most modern and efficient book production techniques and a selective worldwide distribution network—makes available to the academic, government, and business communities significant, timely research in U.S. and international economic, social, and political development.

Desegregating America's Colleges

A Nationwide Survey of Black Students, 1972-73

PRAEGER SPECIAL STUDIES IN U.S. ECONOMIC, SOCIAL, AND POLITICAL ISSUES

Praeger Publishers   New York   Washington   London

Library of Congress Cataloging in Publication Data

Boyd, William M
    Desegregating America's colleges.

    (Praeger special studies in U.S. economic, social, and political issues)
    "Published in cooperation with the Educational Policy Center, inc."
    Includes bibliographical references.
    1. Negroes—Education (Higher) 2. College students, Negro—United States—Statistics. I. Title.
LC2781.B62   378.73   74-5575
ISBN 0-275-09210-0

PRAEGER PUBLISHERS
111 Fourth Avenue, New York, N.Y. 10003, U.S.A.
5, Cromwell Place, London SW7 2JL, England

Published in the United States of America in 1974
by Praeger Publishers, Inc.

Printed in the United States of America

In the sense that any person has been able to find a college or
university to attend in the United States, we have always been able to
say that our country has had an "open system" of higher education.
Over the past decade, moreover, many colleges have been making
extraordinary efforts to open their doors still wider to persons who
have been educationally disadvantaged by reason of financial need,
inadequate preparation, or racial discrimination. And many of these
students are black.

This timely survey of black students in predominantly white
colleges that is the basis for this study by William Boyd, II, provides
us, for the first time, with data on how successful our "openness" has
been. The reporters are 785 black students and 194 faculty members
and administrators. The conclusions that inevitably follow from their
recorded impressions destroy quite a few preconceptions about black
students and their attitudes toward the institutions they attend. Many
readers will be surprised, for instance, that black students feel discrimination most keenly in institutions that have the largest concen-
tration of black students; that black students are apparently more
satisfied with their educational experiences if they attend colleges
in the South; and that, wherever they feel that they are victims of
discrimination, the source is more often believed to be faculty members and administrators than fellow students.

More complicated, and probably more perplexing, is the finding
that black students consider some of the policies for facilitating access
of blacks to institutions of higher education to have serious negative
consequences for them. High on the list of such policies are those
that provide for lower entrance requirements and performance standards without compensating efforts to help those who benefit from such
practices to meet and maintain traditional standards of a college in
a reasonable period of time. Where such policies exist, faculties
and administrators too quickly begin to assume that all black students
on a campus are so educationally handicapped that it would be inap-
propriate to give them the same attention and assistance given to other
students. Even if faculties do not hold such attitudes, black students
may expect them to be present if for no other reason than that they
are, themselves, aware that some black students are not on the same
academic footing as other students on a campus.

The report of such perceptions by black students prompts two
observations that seem particularly well worth remembering. The
first is that there are varying degrees of "openness." A campus

v

may be open in the sense that it is easy to enroll there, but relatively closed in opportunities it provides for black students to participate fully in its programs. The second observation is that there is as much diversity among black students as there is within any other group of students, and that meeting black student needs on a campus may involve less accommodation for what is believed to be the "typical" black student, and more accommodation for the variety of student needs, interests, and abilities to be found among black individuals. It is significant, in this regard, that this report recognizes the usefulness of certain highly publicized campus facilities and channels for social and political adjustment of blacks to the campus mainstream, while stressing as even more important certain programs designed to ease the financial strain under which many black students attend college, to eliminate barriers to intellectual and psychological growth that should be available to all students, and to devise curricula and procedures that demonstrate an awareness of the accomplishments and problems of blacks.

Recently released statistics provided by the American Council on Education suggest that American colleges and universities may be getting ready to back-pedal in their efforts to provide educational opportunities for increasing numbers of blacks and members of other racial minorities. This report of the Educational Policy Center, Inc., may not, of itself, reverse the trend. It should, however, demonstrate in a practical way, why the effort needs to continue and, what is more important, how it might be enhanced and made more effective in the years ahead.

This is an important study on one of the central problems of American higher education, and its recommendations for action are reasonable and deserve both careful study and early implementation.

Clark Kerr
Chairman
Carnegie Council on Policy
Studies in Higher Education

Berkeley, California
March, 1974

A grant from The Ford Foundation made it possible to attempt the study on which this report is based. Successful completion of the study, however, depended on two other factors: the hard work and perseverance of approximately fifty full- and part-time employees of EPC and the cooperation of students, faculty members, and administrators at institutions throughout the country. I appreciate each of those vital contributions.

In addition, I am grateful for the guidance received from members of EPC's Advisory Committee, Board of Directors, and my wife, Arleen, all of whom helped me to isolate and remove a number of weaknesses in the report. If any remain, they are my responsibility.

My greatest thanks go to someone who made no direct contribution to the report. That person is my father, who taught me the crucial importance of equal opportunity in higher education and inspired me, by his example, to struggle for it.

CONTENTS

NATIONAL ADVISORY COMMITTEE

xi

Desegregating America's Colleges

Who knows all about blacks in predominantly white colleges? Unfortunately, no one does. Comprehensive national data of the type that is commonly available for other segments of the college student population never has been gathered about blacks in predominantly white colleges. Many people, therefore, are tempted to act as (or are forced to try to be) "experts." After all, questions about blacks in white colleges are too important to be left unanswered in the 1970s when the majority of black students are attending predominantly white colleges for the first time in history.

These questions also are too important to be answered only on the shaky bases of limited observation and speculation. The Educational Policy Center (EPC) now has developed a firmer basis by going to the most authoritative source available—a nationwide sample of the black students themselves, as well as the faculty members and administrators who work with them. Gathering and analyzing data from these samples has not made us experts, but it has provided some essential and long overdue reference points.

As the debates about equal opportunity in higher education continue, it now will be possible for all of us who participate to share a fund of reliable information. Prospective black students and their parents, college staff members, government officials, philanthropists, and concerned citizens need a common starting point. The data presented here will help all of us to decide whether:

- Current recruiting and admission practices overlook, bypass, and even reject outright very capable black students in favor of less qualified black students who fit a more fashionable stereotype.[1]
- Racial tensions, distrust, some fist fights and a near total segregation in all but classroom activities

characterize the relationships between black and white students. . . .[2]

- From the perspective of the black student . . . the typical white American institution of higher learning is fundamentally unprepared (and in many cases unwilling to be prepared) to meet his needs. From this black standpoint then, it is the institution which should more properly be labeled "high risk."[3]

- The western region is most responsive to the needs of blacks, with the New England region second, the north central and the middle states regions tied for third, the northwest region fifth, and the South clearly last.[4]

To answer questions of this type authoritatively, data needs to come from identifiable and reliable sources through a process which is as objective as possible. The data presented here comes from 979 face-to-face interviews conducted by young, college-educated, black employees of EPC. These interviews, lasting approximately forty-five minutes each, were conducted at forty colleges and universities across the United States during the 1972-73 academic year. There were two groups of respondents: 785 black students and 194 black or white faculty members and administrators. Stratified random sampling techniques were used to assure that the interviews conducted would provide a valid basis for generalizations. The Appendix provides technical details about the selection of colleges and respondents.

The Appendix also contains the questionnaire which was used so that the reader can see the exact wording of questions. This questionnaire was developed after a pre-survey study of students, faculty members, and administrators at six colleges across the country. It should be noted that a great deal of flexibility was built into the final questionnaire by allowing unanticipated responses throughout the interview. These responses were reviewed and coded when the questionnaires were returned. Where it was appropriate, new response categories were added and reported.

To allow as many people as possible to benefit from the survey, this written analysis avoids techniques of analysis which can be understood only by those with backgrounds in statistics. The analysis here is straightforward in dealing only with comparisons of subgroups of respondents. For the same reason, the tables presented in the text and Appendix are as simple and direct as possible.

For those who want to draw their own conclusions, unhindered by the analysis of others, much of the raw data which was compiled is presented in the Appendix. For those who prefer and trust an attempt at objective analysis, the text of the report is available.

For the majority of readers, both the text and the Appendix should be useful.

No matter how thoroughly this report is examined, however, two sets of questions cannot be answered. The first set of questions involves trends. For example, one might ask, "Are predominantly white colleges recruiting larger numbers of poorly prepared black students each year?" Obviously, questions of that type are important, but no one survey of conditions at a single point in time can answer them. EPC will be repeating this study periodically to make it possible to answer these questions.

The second set of questions involves the degree of similarity between the experience of black and white students in areas such as those covered by this study. For example, "Do white students, especially those who legitimately can be classified as 'new students,' share the concern of blacks for greater financial aid and more academic support or even the feeling that they suffer discrimination (economic or ethnic) from staff members?" There is considerable support for such a conclusion in literature and personal observation. Unfortunately, it was not possible to have a control group of white respondents in this year's sample, so conclusive evidence is lacking. When the study is repeated, the plan is to include such a control group. Future surveys will, therefore, provide answers to questions about which we can only speculate now. In what follows here, speculation is kept to a minimum.

NOTES

1. Thomas Sowell, Black Education: Myths And Tragedies (New York: David McKay Company, Inc., 1972), p. 131.

2. Thomas A. Johnson, "Campus Racial Tensions Rise As Black Enrollment Increases," The New York Times, April 4, 1972, p. 1.

3. Gilbert Moore, "The Dot and The Elephant," Change, April 1972, p. 35.

4. Reuben R. McDaniel, Jr. and James W. McKee, An Evaluation of Higher Education's Response to Black Students (Student Association of Higher Education, Indiana University, 1971), p. 4.

2

THE DIVERSITY OF BLACK STUDENTS IN PREDOMINANTLY WHITE COLLEGES

Considering the small amount of data which has been available, a great deal has been said about the characteristics of black students in predominantly white colleges. Many of the statements made have been oversimplified or inaccurate. Their impact has, however, been determined more by the degree to which they fit prevailing racial stereotypes than by their accuracy. The main stereotype is that blacks are so different and deficient that increased equal opportunity in higher education can occur only if colleges lower their academic standards.

Sufficient emphasis is placed on the lack of "qualified" black students to suggest that a picture of a typical student has evolved. He is "Mr. Special Admit:" poor, ill-prepared, in need of remediation, "high risk," in that he is likely to fail (and to demonstrate rather than to fade away quietly), and "street" rather than "middle class" in value system and life style. (Students may be considered "special admits" at any given school because they possess one or any combination of these characteristics.) Once people have become convinced that such students make up most of the "pool" of black aspirants, it has been argued, they bypass students with more standard qualifications in their missionary zeal to help the "real blacks." It also has been argued that they tend to treat all blacks as second-class citizens of the academic community because of the conviction that blacks enter on and should stay on a separate track.

As the various debates become more heated, it appears obvious that more information and less rhetoric are needed. This study provides some of that information. It also documents a point which should be self-evident: all black students are not alike. In fact, EPC's examination of more than one hundred aspects of the background, opinions, and behavior of black students reveals much more diversity than uniformity. It also indicates that statements which begin with "black

students think, feel, are, etc." probably are inaccurate. To be meaningful and accurate such statements must convey characteristics of an
overwhelming majority of the group in question, but in this study large
majorities were rare among black students.* Majorities of 80 percent
or more occur only seven times in responses to EPC's questionnaire.
On ten other occasions majorities of two-thirds or more develop.
Simple majorities occur on twenty-two additional occasions, and no
majority at all exists in response to the remainder of the questions.

In order to understand black students as a nonmonolithic group
and to be able to respond to their needs more effectively, it is necessary to explore in some detail the areas in which great similarities
exist as well as those where great diversity is the rule. This is
particularly important because some of the areas where no majority
exists (including overall dissatisfaction with college and the dominance
of race in all aspects of students' lives) are ones which have been used
as "proof" of uniformity among black students. The areas in which
the largest majorities exist, on the other hand, have received little
attention because they tend to apply equally well to all students regardless of race.

BACKGROUNDS OF BLACK STUDENTS

What statements can legitimately be made about black students
on the basis that they apply to at least 80 percent of them? Black
students are graduates of public high schools (90 percent) and are
not married (91 percent). Most black students go to college in their
home areas, attend and participate in classes at least as much as
other students, and maintain at least a "C" average. They also
indicate that they usually obtain adequate help with their problems
by using some combination of the resources available to them. Based
on EPC's questionnaire, no other sweeping statements about black
students can be made without the qualification that they are not true
for at least one-quarter of that student population.

A number of important characteristics are shared by two-thirds
to three-quarters of black students. Obtaining sufficient funds to
finance a college education is a critical problem. Financial aid
(loans, scholarships, and veterans' benefits) is the primary source
of money for 68 percent of black students (see Table 2.1).

---

*This would not be terribly significant if most of the questions
asked provided a large number of suggested answers for the respond-
ent. In the study, however, many questions had a limited number of
suggested answers or were open ended (see questionnaire in Appendix).

TABLE 2.1

Primary Source of Funds	Percentage of Black Students
Family	20
Scholarship from college	29
Scholarship from other source	16
Loan from college	11
Loan from other source	9
Wages	6
Personal savings	4
Veterans' benefits	3

Note: In some tables in this report, percent totals are less than 100%. This occurs because small numbers of respondents did not or were unable to answer certain questions.

Whatever their primary source of funds is, most black students supplement it by working. Seventy-three percent report that they currently are holding at least one job. In most cases working represents a substantial commitment of time. Although 19 percent work less than ten hours per week, 54 percent work eleven to twenty hours per week, and 20 percent work twenty-one hours or more per week. Table 2.2 shows the location of the students' jobs. Carrying the extra burden of one or more jobs appears to be taken in stride by most black students. Thirty-two percent, however, report that working has a negative impact on their college experience.

Preparation for college also is a problem. Seventy-one percent of black students would prepare differently if they could do it again

TABLE 2.2

Location of Job(s)	Percentage of Black Students
On campus	53
Off campus	35
Both on and off campus	10

so that they could eliminate deficiencies in their high school experience. Table 2.3 indicates the areas of concern of students who feel their preparation was inadequate.

Special favorable treatment is a major issue about which most black students agree. They agree that they do not get any. Sixty-seven percent feel that their college does not really care about having black students. Seventy-three percent say that they receive no "special favorable treatment . . . in any aspects of [their] experience [at the college]." In the specific area of special academic help, slightly fewer (66 percent) say they receive none. Most (79 percent) of those who receive no academic help feel that they need none. Similarly, 76 percent of those who receive academic help feel that it is adequate.

The feeling of academic self-confidence reflected in attitudes toward special academic help can be seen in other responses as well. Seventy-two percent feel there is no likelihood that they will drop out of college. In addition, 72 percent feel that their study habits are as good as or better than those of other students.

Two final statements can be made which apply to two-thirds to three-quarters of black students. Both deal with their experiences with other colleges. Sixty-nine percent have not attended any other college. Sixty-eight percent have considered attending a black college. In half of the cases where students had been enrolled elsewhere, the other institution was a two-year public college. In 39 percent of the cases, the students are transfers from a four-year public (26 percent) or four-year private (13 percent) institution. In 10 percent of the

TABLE 2.3

Areas of Inadequate Preparation	Percentage of Black Students
Math	49
Science	37
English	34
Study habits	17
All areas	17
Writing	15
Reading	13

Note: In some tables in this report, percent totals are more than 100%. This occurs because in some cases multiple responses were possible.

cases the other institution was a traditionally black college. These figures suggest that linkages between two- and four-year institutions are significant but somewhat underdeveloped. They also suggest that transferring is not a major source of "body" or "brain drain" from black to white institutions.

Some remaining distinctions among black students are less dramatic but quite significant. Neither parent of 59 percent of black students attended college. Fifty-six percent come from large cities. The families of 54 percent have incomes of less than $10,000. Fifty-two percent rate their preparation for college as fair or poor. Fifty percent feel that they are "special admits." The fact that approximately one-half of black students do not face the problems which often accompany these statistics is encouraging. On the other hand, there should be great concern for those who do face one or more of these problems.

MAJOR FIELDS AND CAREER PLANS

Background does not determine, but appears to influence strongly, the choice of major fields of interest. Black students continue to follow paths which traditionally have been open to them and which do not penalize them greatly for weaknesses in their preparation. Table 2.4 indicates the most popular majors as well as the amount of interest in several other areas.

Career plans also have a traditional focus. One aspect of this is continuing heavy emphasis on graduate education as a possible technique for making education serve as the ever elusive balance

TABLE 2.4

College Major	Percentage of Black Students
Social Sciences	28
Business	15
Education	15
Biological Sciences	6
English	4
Engineering and Math	4
Physical Sciences	2
Black Studies	1

wheel that can place blacks on an equal footing with whites. More than half of black college students aspire to graduate education either full-time (45 percent) or along with work (10 percent). It appears likely that many of these aspirations will be unfulfilled because only 26 percent of black students have average grades of "B" or above. No doubt many of the unrealistic aspirants would be less interested in obtaining graduate credentials if blacks were able to obtain satisfying jobs and earn as much as whites without having several years more education. (Source: Bureau of Labor Statistics income figures as reported in Jet, August 26, 1971: Average annual income for a white man with a college education—$8,829. Average annual income for a black man with a college education—$8,669.)

Among those planning to go to graduate school, 10 percent plan to pursue Ph.D. degrees. In general, preferences for graduate study cluster in a few familiar fields: law (21 percent), medicine (21 percent), social sciences (18 percent), education (9 percent), and business (7 percent). Among those planning to go directly to work, the pattern is similar. Education and business are the dominant preferences, with approximately one-quarter of the students leaning toward each.

The pattern of specialization which is evident among black students generates some concern when one considers projections of decreased job opportunities in fields such as education and social sciences and increased job opportunities in scientific and technical fields such as engineering. In addition, it suggests that educators who feel that the limited option syndrome no longer is a problem should reexamine their conclusions. Black students simply are not taking advantage of the entire range of options available. This in turn raises questions about the type of exposure to varied options and the type of guidance being offered to black students. Responses to EPC's survey demonstrate that this area merits considerable attention.

Table 2.5 indicates that black students seek advice about jobs and careers from a variety of sources. It shows, however, that 20 percent seek no advice at all as they make decisions in this critical area. That group is more than twice as large as the groups which try to handle academic or financial problems without assistance. Unfortunately, this is not the result of a very high percentage of lower classmen mingled with a low percentage of upper classmen. The figures for first- through fourth-year students are as follows: 19 percent, 20 percent, 23 percent, and 17 percent respectively.

Those students who seek help rely most on counselors and, in particular, on black counselors. Clearly, many black students are obtaining no advice or advice only from young and inexperienced staff members. This means that these students are not benefiting from the help of some of the most knowledgeable people on campus. Table 2.5 also suggests that few students are seeking advice from several

TABLE 2.5

Sources of Advice on Jobs/Careers	Percentage of Black Students
Black counselors	23
White counselors	13
Black administrators	12
White administrators	16
Black faculty members	12
White faculty members	11
Family	13
No one	20

sources. If more students were consulting several sources, the total percentage of responses would be considerably higher than it is,

REACTIONS TO COLLEGES

Interaction with the institution or segments of it produces a majority viewpoint among black students on several subjects. Although some of the agreement reflects strong criticism of their colleges, the majority's overall reaction to their college experience is not negative. Sixty-four percent are at least somewhat satisfied. Curriculum is the only characteristic of colleges which prompts a positive reaction from a majority (62 percent) of black students. Probably more students would be satisfied if they obtained better information and counseling before choosing a college. Even with allowances for the influence of factors such as college costs and the proximity of a college to a student's home, a substantial majority of students also should be able to satisfy themselves in terms of the setting, average class size, and supportive services of a given college. This is not, however, the case as none of these characteristics is given a positive rating by a majority of black students. The percentages for setting (urban or rural), size of classes, and supportive services are 42, 42, and 38 percent respectively.

Characteristics of their colleges which are listed as having negative impact by 60 percent of the students are deficiencies in: percentage of black enrollment, percentage of blacks in the faculty and administration, and overt attempts to be responsive to the needs of blacks. It is understandable that students find it difficult to satisfy

10

themselves in terms of these characteristics. There are, after all, few predominantly white colleges which have changed enough to please blacks with their recruitment or responsiveness.

Two other characteristics of colleges which are perceived by a majority of black students could have negative consequences but apparently do not. Intense academic competition is felt by 59 percent, and a majority of that group (62 percent) feel it has had an effect on them. The nature of the effect appears to be the key factor: students are motivated to work harder much more frequently than to lose their self-confidence or ability to function. In response to a question about the ability of black students "to influence the programs of [their] college that affect . . . life as a student," 64 percent felt they had no such ability. This has less negative impact than it might because 57 percent gave positive answers to a question about the ability of black students to "influence programs of [their] college through organized group efforts."

The final two areas in which a majority of black students agree involve such slight majorities that it probably is more accurate to say that opinion is evenly divided. Racial discrimination has not been a part of the experience of 51 percent of the students. Fifty-three percent have no concern about their "ability to meet the costs of [their] college education."

Reaction to these statistics must be as mixed as the numbers themselves. There is much that is encouraging, but all of it has a significant discouraging aspect. For example, there clearly is no room for unbridled joy about the fact that very close to one-half of all black students are worried about their ability to continue to meet the costs of their education. In addition, it is indeed sad that a similar number feel they are victims of racial discrimination. The reported discrimination is particularly distressing because it most often involves treatment by faculty members. Table 2.6 contains a list of the types of discrimination cited most frequently.

The types of discrimination cited by black students within the broad categories listed in Table 2.6 are quite varied, but there are some recurring themes. The major problems between black students and faculty members involve assumptions about black students, behavior toward black students, and remarks to or about blacks. Many black students feel that professors view them as incompetents. For example, a student said a professor "told me I would probably need special help without knowing me or my abilities." The students feel that this injects self-fulfilling prophecy, if not outright inequality, into the grading process. Grades then tend to be lower than performance would dictate.

Students also criticize a tendency to assume they are dishonest. Examples given include refusing to let black students sit together

11

TABLE 2.6

Types of Discrimination	Percentage of Black Students
Treatment by faculty (grading, treatment in class, accessibility outside class)	42
Subtle manifestations (attitudes, lack of respect, tendency to overlook blacks)	21
Different standards of behavior for blacks	13
Overt manifestations (comments, remarks, attempts to avoid proximity)	11
Harassment by police/guards	8

during exams and questioning whether black students actually wrote term papers they submitted merely because the papers were outstanding. Other faculty behavior which is criticized includes being accessible outside class only to white students, accusing black students who seek additional help of wanting "handouts" or "everything on a silver platter," and ignoring or slighting black students in class. Finally, there are two types of behavior which are all too familiar: calling white students "Mr." or "Miss" but using the first names of black students, and "expecting blacks to have all the answers to racial problems or feeling that [they] are completely stupid."

In referring to discrimination from people other than faculty members, black students distinguish overt from subtle types. Overt discrimination includes such things as calling them "niggers," refusing to cash checks or money orders, "vulgar remarks about white men and black women," criticizing blacks for behavior while ignoring the same behavior by whites, and refusing to accept assignment of a black roommate or lab partner.

Subtle discrimination does not involve direct confrontation or exchange, but concerns such things as the college newspaper's not covering black events, administrators giving students the runaround rather than the help they need, not enough counseling, "coldness and condescension," and "a general attitude of white supremacy." As one student summarized the situation, the problem is "disrespect twenty-four hours a day."

Much of the controversy about black students in predominantly white colleges focuses on issues which have not yet been mentioned here. Major examples of this involve extended discussions of the social maladjustment, anti-intellectualism, or separatism of black students. The reasons for their omission is clear: they do not involve a majority of black students. The reasons for their prominence elsewhere is less clear. Debating the good or bad intentions of various people who have popularized myths about "where black students are at" is not a concern here. It should be noted, however, that the absence of reliable data has encouraged extravagant rhetoric and ill-advised actions. Hopefully, the information gathered by this study will encourage people to build on more reliable foundations as they attempt to provide equal opportunity for blacks in higher education.

SEPARATISM

Separatism is the balloon in which the largest amount of hot air has collected. It is now quite common for whites and blacks to assert that blacks want to withdraw as completely as possible from contact with whites and should be allowed or encouraged to do so while remaining in predominantly white institutions. Black dorms, black student organizations, black tables or areas in the student union, Black Studies, and the like have provided ample evidence for some that most black students are separatists. Institutional climates designed around false assumptions may lead to a situation in which most black students become separatists. At present, however, there is evidence that separatism is a minority viewpoint among black students.

All-black housing has been the most overemphasized and misinterpreted issue among those associated with separatism. It is overemphasized because only one percent of black students indicate that a change in their housing would improve their college experience. The misinterpretation is especially obvious in arguments urging black dorms for all black students when, in fact, neither a black dormitory nor any other type of housing is preferred by a majority of black students. Table 2.7, which indicates actual and preferred living arrangements, should clarify the current situation.

Additional perspective is provided by the reasons for preferring a certain type of housing. By far the most popular (34 percent) revolves around "freedom, independence, privacy, solitude, or quiet." Two reasons are tied as the next most popular at 10 percent: maximum contact/understanding with other blacks, and maximum contact/ understanding with whites. Obviously, an arrangement which provides only one housing option for black students is undesirable.

Attitudes and behavior around the campus are the other major aspect of the separatism which has been attributed to black students. Naturally, in a setting where almost half the black students experience racial discrimination, race will be a factor in the choice of friends and activities. Nevertheless, only four out of ten black students

13

TABLE 2.7

	Housing (by percent)	
	Actual	Preferred
Dorm that mixes whites and blacks	48	20
All-black or minority dorm, floor, or wing	4	15
Private, off-campus apartment or room	24	46
Parents' home	18	9

indicate that it is a dominant factor. Similarly, 47 percent participate in black organizations on campus, but participation also is significant in athletics (30 percent), general student activities such as "club, choir, or newspaper," (25 percent), and student government (11 percent).

Relationships with faculty members is another area where separatism allegedly manifests itself. There are few black faculty members and administrators at predominantly white colleges, but they are "most influential" on 30 percent of black students. That is interesting but hardly convincing evidence of widespread separatism. In addition, there is a readily apparent alternate explanation for the limited influence of whites. Forty-two percent of the black students who feel discriminated against list the faculty as the source of discrimination. This is twice as large as the number listing the second most frequent type of discrimination. Thus it appears that white faculty behavior contributes as much to their limited influence as any ideology held by black students.

One other myth which is not related to separatism should be discussed. Its basis is the idea that the majority of black students want special treatment ("positive discrimination") and that it is a big favor to extend it to them. A variation on the theme is that everyone else is doing it, and if you don't, you're a racist/Uncle Tom. Actually, only one-quarter of the black students feel they are receiving special treatment, and their reactions to it are mixed: 34 percent react positively, 28 percent react negatively, 14 percent are ambivalent, and 12 percent feel little or no reaction.

LACK OF DIVERSITY

In spite of all the evidence of diversity among black students, it must be remembered that myths like the one about their uniformity

14

usually are organized around a germ of truth. It, therefore, is important to look for an example of the monolithic, stereotypical black student body and to examine it closely. No college exactly fits the special admit syndrome described earlier, but some come close. Fifty-five percent of predominantly white colleges have a majority of black students (as large as 85 percent) who identify themselves as special entrants. In 15 percent of these institutions, neither parent of a majority of black students attended college. Twelve percent of the colleges have a majority of black students from families with incomes under $10,000. Loans are the primary source of financial support for a majority of the black special entrants at 20 percent of the colleges.

Fortunately, there is a limited amount of overlap in these categories, so few colleges have a majority of their black students burdened with multiple disadvantages (inadequate preparation, poverty, "cultural deprivation," and the absence of college-educated persons in one's immediate family). Eighteen percent do have a majority of black students who are special admits whose parents did not attend college. Eight percent have a majority of black students who are special admits whose parents did not attend college and whose family income is under $10,000. Only 2 percent have a majority of black students who are special admits, whose parents did not attend college, whose family income is under $10,000, and who are supporting themselves primarily by loans.

The profile of a college where the majority of black students are multiply disadvantaged and relying on loans is instructive. At this college 70 percent of the black students are dissatisfied with their overall college experience (versus a national norm of 64 percent who are at least somewhat satisfied). Seventy percent are influenced by no faculty member of administrator (national norm: 24 percent). Seventy percent participate in black organizations (national norm: 47 percent). Eighty-five percent perceive intense academic competition (national norm: 59 percent). Thirty-five percent estimate the attrition rate at the college to be 50 percent or more (nationally only 9 percent make such a high estimate of attrition).

To test your own attitudes about equal opportunity in higher education, try to describe a college which has every element of the incredibly negative syndrome described above. In what part of the country is it located? Is it public or private? Is it large or small? Does it have low, medium, or high black enrollment? Is it a northeastern, private, small, low black enrollment college? Is it a southern, public, large, medium black enrollment college? Actually, the college in question is in the West. It is a less selective, large, public institution with low black enrollment.

A comparison with a similar college in the West is interesting. It also is public and large. A majority of its black students are special admits from families with incomes under $10,000. Forty percent of its black students come from families where neither parent attended college. Only 20 percent, however, rely on loans as their primary source of financial support. Other differences between the colleges may account for some of the contrasts in the climate at the two schools, but the lower number receiving loans and having multiple disadvantages certainly appears significant.

At the second college, which is more selective, the black students are much closer to the national norms in key areas. Only 35 percent are dissatisfied. Twenty-five percent are influenced by no faculty member or administrator. Thirty percent participate in black organizations. Eighty-five percent perceive intense academic competition, but only 5 percent estimate the attrition rate to be 50 percent or more.

One can argue that it is an honest, though racist, mistake for a predominantly white college to cater almost exclusively to multiply disadvantaged black students as if it believes no other kind exists. Once data of the type presented here is available, however, colleges which pursue such a course will appear to have little or no concern for the academic success and personal growth which are the essence of equal opportunity in higher education. Racist rhetoric which argues that this is the only way to serve large numbers of blacks can now be seen for what it is. Some middle class blacks are disadvantaged intellectually, and many poorer blacks are not multiply disadvantaged.

There is no valid reason for operating, as some colleges appear to have done, on the assumption that all blacks from well-to-do families have good academic potential and all blacks from poorer families have little academic potential but deserve a break. Many students and some "experts" already have concluded that the willingness or eagerness of some colleges to enroll large numbers of multiply disadvantaged blacks is avaricious and/or malicious. These students and staff members argue that such colleges are interested only in "body count" in dealing with black students and government funds for them. They also contend that such colleges are concerned about failure among blacks only to the extent that they want to cover it up to maintain their access to funds for the disadvantaged.

Whatever the explanation for such policies, it is clear that they reinforce racist stereotypes present among whites at the college while aggravating frustration and alienation among young blacks. It also is clear that understanding and improving the experience of black students in predominantly white colleges are difficult undertakings. Careful attention to the information and analysis presented here should contribute significantly to those efforts.

3

CHARACTERISTICS OF
BLACK STUDENTS

National averages such as the ones presented here are important but limited. Without them it is impossible to put information about regions, types of colleges, and the like in perspective. Like any averages, however, they may result from the combination of very similar or very diverse elements. An average of 50 percent nationally might result from combining figures for public and private colleges which were 51 percent and 49 percent. The same 50 percent national average also could result from combining public and private college figures of 75 percent and 25 percent. It, therefore, is important to look behind national averages for factors which relate to or explain variations from the national norm.

To understand fully the experience of black students in predominantly white colleges, one must answer a question which is more specific than questions about all black students as a group:—"Do observable characteristics of students or colleges such as sex and socioeconomic status or level of black enrollment and location make a difference?" This chapter and the next one attempt to answer that question. Because the possibility of variation is so great, a difference which makes no difference in one setting may make a significant difference in another setting. For example, the fact that only a few black faculty members and administrators are employed may have a considerably different impact on students in colleges where there are few black students than on those where there is a high level of black enrollment.

To identify the differences that make a difference, one needs to consider a number of variables. Some of them have received a great deal of attention from other observers, and some have not. Obviously, it has been difficult to know where to place emphasis without having national norms as a guide. Now that the norms are available, it should be possible to rely less on intuition and participant observation as bases for deciding which aspects of the experience of black students in predominantly white colleges are most significant.*

SEX

EPC's study identifies several significant differences between black males and females at predominantly white colleges. These differences involve, almost exclusively, family and educational background as well as academic behavior and opinions related to background. The differences are similar to those between white women and white men. Black women at predominantly white colleges tend to come from more highly educated and richer families than black men. Twice as many females (22 percent) as males (11 percent) indicate that both their parents attended college. Fifty percent of the females and 66 percent of the males say neither parent attended college. Twenty-three percent of the females versus 15 percent of the males report family incomes of $15,000 or more. As a result, more than twice as many females (30 percent) as males (12 percent) have their families as their primary source of financial support.

Black women appear to do better academically than black men. Fewer females (46 percent) than males (56 percent) report fair or poor academic preparation for college. Females perform better academically in college, with 31 percent, versus 21 percent for males, obtaining "B" averages. In addition, slightly more females (58 percent) plan to attend graduate school.

Black women also have more contact with faculty members outside of class, but that does not appear to be altogether a positive experience. Forty-four percent of the males, versus 35 percent of the females, have little or no contact with faculty members. Women see faculty members slightly more about classwork and job or career prospects, substantially more about extra projects, and twice as much about general academic subjects. The negative side of the picture is that females (49 percent) identify faculty members as a source of discrimination more than males (37 percent) do.

The overall pattern of differences between males and females suggests the existence of a pitfall which should be avoided by colleges. It is possible for colleges to have a large gap separating their black male and female students while maintaining good overall academic

---

*Treating these factors separately is not intended to obscure possible relationships between them or to imply a unilateral causal relationship between a given factor (like sex) and a given observation (like better preparation for college).

18

statistics. That kind of gap, however, probably creates great tensions among the black student population and is not a viable or desirable long-term strategy. It is not difficult to conclude that young men tend to be threatened by and ill at ease with young women who are more effective academically and socially. One way to deal with this problem without admitting it, is to attack not black women, but bourgeois blacks. If a college allows the two to become virtually synonomous, it is asking for trouble.

The development of such a gap also rests upon and contributes to the matriarchal stereotype of black women as "ants" (encouragingly middle class) and black men as "grasshoppers" (pathologically lower class). The stereotype can be put in perspective by recruiting black men and women who are similar in background. Under those circumstances the two groups produce similar results, and a more realistic view of the distribution of talent and energy among blacks emerges.

COLLEGE GENERATION

Just as EPC's data partially confirms the stereotype of females as better students, it partially confirms the stereotype of the black who is the first in his or her family to attend college. That student's family is more likely to have an income under $10,000 (69 percent) than is the family of a student whose parents have some college education (46 percent). The first generation student, therefore, is more likely to require substantial amounts of financial aid. Seventy-eight percent of first generation students (63 percent of those with prior college in the family) report that financial aid is their main source of funds. In addition, it is more likely that the first generation student has to work twenty-one hours or more per week to make ends meet. Thirty percent of first generation students (14 percent of other students) indicated that they have this type of work schedule.

First generation students are less likely to have had good academic preparation. Fifty-six percent of first generation students (49 percent of those with prior college in the family) feel that they have fair or poor academic preparation. First generation students also worry more (35 percent to 28 percent) about cutbacks in special programs for blacks.

On the other hand, it is not true that first generation black students are different in their values and behavior from other black students. They do not pursue different majors, participate in different activities, or even prefer different types of housing. In addition, it appears that they are no more involved with race as an issue than other black students. Thirty-six percent (versus 44 percent of other

black students) say race is the dominant factor in their choice of
friends and activities. Forty-one percent (versus 53 percent) have
been victims of racial discrimination, and 35 percent (versus 44 percent) of that group identify the faculty as the source of discrimination.

SOCIOECONOMIC STATUS

It can be argued that one of the important steps taken by a college aspirant is being born into a family with money. Chances of
attending college are dramatically better for students whose family
income is $16,000 than those whose family income is $4,000. Table
3.1 indicates the extent to which EPC's study suggests such a relationship between family income and college attendance.

TABLE 3.1

| | Percentage Blacks In: | | Percentage All Groups In:[†] | |
| | General Population* | White Colleges | General Population | White Colleges |
Family Income	(1971)	(1972)	(1971)	(1971)
$0—4,999	38	18	23	14
$5,000—9,999	34	36	36	32
$10,000—14,999	17	25	25	27
$15,000 and over	11	19	16	27

Source: *Money Income In 1971 of Families and Persons in the
United States, U.S. Department of Commerce, Bureau of the Census,
December, 1972, p. 70.
          †Iver Peterson, "Carnegie Panel Bids Middle Class
Pay Bigger Share of College Cost," The New York Times, July 13,
1973, p. 10.

Several characteristics of black students are related to family
income. Students from families with higher incomes are less likely
to have: parents who did not attend college, fair or poor preparation,
special admissions status, or financial aid as a primary source of
funds. Table 3.2 indicates the degree to which money changes the
odds.

The financial aid picture is more complex than the table suggests.
Reliance on scholarships does decrease steadily with increases in

TABLE 3.2

| | Family Income of Black Students (by percent) | | | |
	$0— 4,999	$5,000— 9,999	$10,000— 14,999	$15,000+
Neither parent attended college	76	73	52	23
Fair or poor preparation	58	53	48	47
Special admit	57	55	50	35
Financial aid as primary source of funds	90	76	67	34

income from 62 percent of those in the lowest income category to 22 percent of those in the highest. Loans do not, however, follow a logical pattern. Unfortunately, the poorest students have the second highest (24 percent) reliance on loans. Those in the $10,000—14,999 category are most heavily reliant on loans (28 percent), with the $5,000—9,999 and $15,000 and over groups third (19 percent) and last (11 percent) respectively. Worry about increasing debt is an additional burden which should not fall so heavily on the poorest students. As the sketch of the multiproblem college indicates, this can hinder both academic and social adjustment. Clearly, more effort is needed to reduce or eliminate borrowing as the major means of financing education for the most economically disadvantaged students.

Four other important characteristics neither increase nor decrease steadily as family income increases. In fact, with regard to three of these characteristics, the lowest income category is closer to the highest income category than to either of the other categories. Table 3.3 illustrates this pattern.

The poorest and the richest students are most likely to be found at colleges at some distance from their homes. They also tend to be more dissatisfied with their overall college experience. This appears to relate to two specific areas of their experience. They are more likely to feel that faculty members discriminate against them and are more likely to participate in black student organizations.

It is understandable that being far from home adds to the difficulty of adjusting to college. It also appears evident that the adjustment should be more difficult for poorer students who probably have had less experience with campus and boarding schools and have fewer opportunities to stay in contact with family and friends through telephone conversations and visits. Colleges, therefore, should make every effort not to add additional problems to the load carried by poorer students who are far from home. Financial and other types of assistance should be ample, timely, and predictable.

COLLEGE YEAR

The variables discussed so far are ones which do not change (sex) or are unlikely to change (parents' education and income category) during a student's college years. Variables which do change or can change significantly, therefore, can provide additional insight. An example of this is a student's college year. Are first-year students different from fourth-year students? If so, what causes the differences? At this point, EPC's data provides answers to the first question. It cannot, however, provide definitive answers to the second until EPC has repeated the study. Any observed differences, and there are several, which suggest that students are more displeased in each class year could be related to positive or negative developments. It is possible that fourth-year students are the most unhappy group because the cumulative effect of attending white colleges is negative and depressing. It is equally possible, however, that fourth-year students

TABLE 3.3

	Family Income of Black Students (by percent)			
	$0—4,999	$5,000—9,000	$10,000—14,999	$15,000+
College in home area	67	84	81	74
Somewhat or very satisfied	56	68	65	63
Faculty as source of discrimination	57	37	37	43
Participation in black student organization	51	45	42	59

are the most unhappy group because the Class of '73 was the first big contingent of blacks on many campuses. They may have faced and been soured by pioneering problems that are being reduced each year. Speculation about which explanation is more likely does not appear to be a fruitful exercise, so this report simply reports the current situation. In reports on subsequent studies, comparison with the data here will make it possible to move beyond speculation.

Table 3.4 suggests that either the pool of black candidates for college is improving or that predominantly white colleges are becoming more adept at tapping that pool.

TABLE 3.4

| | College Year (by percent) | | | |
	1st	2nd	3rd	4th
Neither parent attended college	52	57	64	65
No sibling attended college	47	55	54	67
Fair/Poor preparation	47	57	46	56
Special admit	44	50	54	54

The most recent entrants are less likely to be the first members of their immediate families to attend college. They also are less likely to feel that they are burdened by poor preparation or that they are special admits. Before reaching conclusions, however, two things must be considered. Not all students who have prior college in their families are better academic prospects than those who do not. In addition, opinions about adequacy of preparation and special circumstances of admissions may change, especially during the second year (or "sophomore slump").

For whatever reasons, students who have been in college longer are more negative about their college experience. Table 3.5 makes this clear.

TABLE 3.5

| | College Year (by percent) | | | |
	1st	2nd	3rd	4th
Somewhat or very satisfied	76	64	59	54
College doesn't care about blacks	56	68	73	72
No racial discrimination	64	54	49	36
Less financial aid each year	28	39	41	60

More students in each college year are dissatisfied, and fewer feel that the college cares about having blacks there. More students in each college year have experienced racial discrimination, and fewer feel confident that the financial aid "pie" is not shrinking.

4

CHARACTERISTICS OF
COLLEGES

Looking at the college experience of black students in terms of characteristics possessed by those students is revealing. It is not, however, a sufficient technique for isolating factors which contribute to or detract from a successful educational experience. Consideration of student characteristics, therefore, must be supplemented by examination of characteristics of colleges.

SPONSORSHIP

One would expect college characteristics to have great impact, and they do. This is true even though many popular ways of grouping colleges, like ways of categorizing students, produce groups which are characterized by only a limited number of similar traits. Dividing colleges according to public or private sponsorship is an example. The differences between the experience of blacks at public and private colleges are significant, but the list does not include some old standbys like more contact with faculty at private colleges.

In the critical area of admissions and financial assistance, there are important differences between public and private colleges. More students at public colleges (86 percent) are in their home area than are those at private colleges (63 percent). Fewer students feel that they are special admits at public (46 percent) than at private (59 percent) colleges. Not surprisingly, reliance on financial aid is more frequent at private (72 percent) than public (66 percent) colleges, and the aid is more often scholarships than loans at private (55 percent) than at public (40 percent) colleges.

The overall climate at the colleges is not as different as it is in stereotypes, but there are substantial differences. Public colleges are perceived as less responsive to the needs of blacks by a 64 percent to 55 percent margin. Their faculties are identified as a source of discrimination more frequently (45 percent versus 35 percent). Somewhat offsetting these negative characteristics of public colleges is their better record in employing black faculty members and administrators. Sixty-nine percent of black students at private colleges feel that more needs to be done in employment (versus 56 percent at public colleges). More students at private colleges participate in all extracurricular activities, including black organizations.

Analysis of transfer patterns of black students provides several interesting distinctions between public and private colleges. Table 4.1 indicates the distribution of students who previously have been enrolled at another college.

TABLE 4.1

Previous College	Current College (by percent)	
	Public	Private
Two-year public college	57	32
Black college	13	5
Four-year public college	23	34
Four-year private college	10	18

Obviously, public colleges draw more heavily on community colleges and black colleges as sources of students than private colleges do. On the other hand, private colleges obtain the majority of their black transfer students from other white four-year institutions.

LEVEL OF BLACK ENROLLMENT

As the experience of blacks in predominantly white colleges has become more extensive, a kind of critical mass theory has evolved. This theory argues that there must be a substantial number of blacks on a given campus to provide sufficient opportunities for satisfactory adjustment.[1] The theory is based on the obvious psychological and social strains placed on highly visible, small groups of minority students. EPC's data supports the general argument about the relationship between the relative number of blacks in a given situation and the ease of adjustment. For example, in colleges with low black enrollment, unlike in those with medium or high, problems like isolation and frustration are seen as the main reasons for attrition.

One-third of the students who say there is some likelihood that they will drop out give an "inhospitable campus environment" as the reason.

One vital qualification, however, is necessary. Unless colleges make adjustments in a number of areas, there are disadvantages associated with high black enrollment which offset some of the advantages. The other side of the critical mass coin is that blacks in large numbers are more likely to be perceived as a threat. More effort, therefore, has to be directed at eliminating on-campus discrimination as admissions discrimination decreases. Table 4.2 demonstrates that the extent and type of discrimination are different in colleges with low black enrollment and those with medium or high black enrollment.

TABLE 4.2

	Black Enrollment (by percent)		
	Low	Medium	High
No racial discrimination	64	47	50
Overt discrimination			
(remarks, etc.)	22	10	11
Faculty discrimination	24	46	43

There is more discrimination in general where there are more black students. The sources of it, however, are different in that less comes from other students and more comes from faculty members.

Level of enrollment also is associated with other differences in the college experience of blacks. Where there are few blacks, more of them feel that the college cares about them and is responsive to their needs. This is true even though greater numbers do give black students a greater sense of power. Table 4.3 provides data on these points.

It is possible that all the differences associated with enrollment levels are more directly related to other characteristics of colleges such as size, location, and sponsorship. EPC's data, however, provides no strong evidence that this is the case. As Table 4.4 indicates, there is widespread distribution of the various enrollment levels.

Only one comment about enrollment levels and types of colleges appears necessary. Since no southern colleges have high black enrollment, it is possible that the positive profile which they present (see discussion of region later in this chapter) will change. It also is possible that, being forewarned, they can avoid the negative repercussions associated with high black enrollment elsewhere.

TABLE 4.3

| | Black Enrollment (by percent) | | |
	Low	Medium	High
College doesn't care about black students	57	70	68
Negative reaction to responsiveness of college	53	58	65
Ability of black students to influence programs	46	67	55

TABLE 4.4

| | Black Enrollment | | |
	Low	Medium	High
National Norm	16	30	54
Region			
NE	7	19	74
MW	5	28	67
S	38	62	—
W	24	—	76
Sponsorship			
Public	16	23	61
Private	16	44	39
Size			
Small	16	36	48
Medium	17	29	54
Large	15	25	59
Location*			
MU	8	42	50
OU	20	12	67
NM	25	52	23

*Major Urban (MU), other Urban (OU), Non-metropolitan (NM)

LOCATION

Being in a large or small city or a non-metropolitan area makes a substantial difference to black students. As Table 4.4 shows, location is related to level of black enrollment, with larger concentrations of black students being found in major urban or other urban areas. (Our divisions are as follows: major urban, central cities with a population of 100,000 or more and their suburban rings; other urban, areas with a population of 20,000-99,999; non-metropolitan, areas with a population of under 20,000.) The reactions of blacks to the location of their college indicate that this pattern is likely to continue. Location of the college is seen as a negative characteristic by 46 percent of those in non-metropolitan colleges, 30 percent of those in other urban colleges, and only 13 percent of those in major urban colleges. In addition, many more students at non-metropolitan colleges are away from their home area. Percentages of those who remain in their home area are as follows: 80 percent in major urban, 85 percent in other urban, and 50 percent in non-metropolitan colleges.

Academic performance is another problem at non-metropolitan colleges because 19 percent of the black students have "D" and "F" averages (versus 5 percent in both other types of colleges). Finally, the shortage of black faculty members and administrators at non-metropolitan colleges inhibits black enrollment. Seventy-six percent of those in non-metropolitan colleges identify it as a problem, versus 64 percent in other urban and 51 percent in major urban colleges.

Overall evaluations of college experience follow this pattern, but the differences are less pronounced. The percentage of somewhat satisfied or very satisfied is as follows: 70 percent in major urban, 60 percent in other urban, and 58 percent in non-metropolitan colleges. Obviously, therefore, there are characteristics which increase the attractiveness of non-metropolitan schools. They include less feeling that the college does not care, fewer special admits, and more favorable reaction to class size.

Other urban colleges are almost tied with non-metropolitan colleges in terms of overall dissatisfaction among black students. Several possible causes of that dissatisfaction can be identified. Other urban colleges have the greatest percentage (54 percent) of special admits. They also have the largest percentage (37 percent, versus 26 percent and 23 percent in major urban and non-metropolitan colleges) who are worried about the impact of cutbacks in special programs on their financial situation. Finally, other urban colleges are first in percentage of students who feel that the college does not care about them.

Major urban colleges appear to have the best academic atmo-
sphere. They have more students with "B" averages than do other
types of colleges (30 percent, versus 24 percent in other urban and
17 percent in non-metropolitan colleges). Major urban colleges also
have more diversity in major fields among their black students.
Table 4.5 indicates that major urban students are well represented
in all fields including the technical and scientific ones. This is not
the case in other urban and non-metropolitan colleges where 50 percent and 46 percent of blacks are in social sciences and education.

TABLE 4.5

| | Location of College (by percent) | | |
| | Major | Other | Non-metro- |
Major Field	Urban	Urban	politan
Social Sciences	25	32	24
Education	10	18	22
Business	18	11	15
Biological Sciences	10	3	2
Engineering and Math	7	2	-
Physical Sciences	1	3	-
English	4	3	5
Fine Arts	4	5	6
Black Studies	1	1	-

Major urban colleges appear to provide the best experience
for black students in all major areas of concern except one: financial
aid. When the list of changes which would "improve the experience
of black students here" is examined, only financial aid, relevant curriculum, and more involvement in decision making are emphasized
more strongly by major urban students than by those at other types
of colleges. Table 4.6 provides information about changes desired
by black students.

SELECTIVITY

A common and important way of looking at colleges is to cate-
gorize them according to selectivity.[2] Examining more selective
colleges is extremely useful to an analysis of the experience of black
students in predominantly white colleges. Black students in more

TABLE 4.6

Changes Desired	Location of College (by percent)			
	Nat'l. Norm	Major Urban	Other Urban	Non-metro-politan
More recruitment of blacks	59	53	60	77
More financial aid, especially for blacks	41	47	38	34
Expansion of Black Studies	33	25	33	55
More remedial programs and tutoring	24	23	28	13
Purge of racists from staff	15	13	11	33
More black activities, social life, culture	14	10	18	17
More "relevance" in curriculum	5	7	4	2
Revised admissions standards	4	4	4	-
Greater role in decision making	4	7	3	2
Black lounge or center	1	2	1	-
All-black housing	1	2	-	1

selective colleges are different in significant ways from those in less selective colleges. There also are major differences in the way black students are treated in more selective colleges. And, not surprisingly, there are marked differences between the reactions and performance of black students attending more selective colleges and those attending less selective colleges.

The backgrounds of black students in more selective colleges vary considerably from those of black students in less selective colleges. Family income and educational levels tend to be higher in more selective colleges as Table 4.7 indicates. It is interesting to note, however, that the middle income ($10,000—14,999) group is similar to the lowest income group in being less well represented in more selective colleges than in less selective ones.

Background characteristics other than those associated directly with family also distinguish students in more selective colleges. More students in those colleges (66 percent, versus 53 percent in less selective colleges) come from large cities. Slightly fewer come

TABLE 4.7

	College (by percent)	
	More	Less
Family Income	Selective	Selective
$0-4,999	10	20
$5,000-9,999	40	35
$10,000-14,999	21	26
$15,000-24,999	17	12
$25,000 and over	6	6
Parents' College Education		
Both parents	22	14
Father only	10	10
Mother only	16	15
Neither parent	50	62

from small cities, suburban areas, and rural areas. The feeling
that previous academic preparation was excellent or good is expressed
by a greater percentage of students in more selective colleges (59
percent) than in less selective colleges (45 percent). In other words,
more selective schools do appear to attract black students with better
academic backgrounds. More selective colleges also enroll fewer
black students (20 percent, versus 26 percent in less selective colleges) who have transferred from another institution. While the
relative numbers may not be surprising, there are some surprises
in the sources of the transfers (see Table 4.8).

TABLE 4.8

	Current College (by percent)	
	More	Less
Previous College	Selective	Selective
Two-year public college	63.0	46
Two-year private college	.5	6
Black college	.5	11
Four-year public college	46.0	21
Four-year private college	.5	14

Clearly, less selective colleges attract transfers from junior colleges, black colleges, and four-year private colleges, while almost all transfers at more selective colleges come from community colleges or four-year public colleges. This suggests that many of those from community colleges and four-year public colleges who do transfer want to finish at the best possible institution.

Students in more selective colleges not only are different from those in less selective colleges, but they also are treated differently. In the crucial area of financial aid, students at more selective colleges are more likely to obtain scholarships sufficient to provide their primary source of funds and to have those scholarships come from the college itself (see Table 4.9).

TABLE 4.9

Primary Source of Funds	College (by percent)	
	More Selective	Less Selective
Family	18	21
Scholarship from college	45	24
Scholarship from other source	11	17
Loan from college	6	12
Loan from bank	6	6
Loan from other source	2	3
Personal savings	1	5
Wages	5	6
Veterans' benefits	2	3

This greater reliance on scholarships allows students at more selective colleges to avoid heavy debts. It also reduces the need to work while attending college. Eighty-two percent of students at less selective colleges hold jobs, while only 42 percent of those at more selective colleges do.

More selective and less selective colleges also differ on the amount and type of discrimination to which black students are exposed. More students feel they have been victims of discrimination at more selective colleges (53 percent) than at less selective colleges (48 percent). The discrimination, however, is less likely to come from faculty members and less likely to be overt (see Table 4.10).

Students in more selective colleges are more likely to receive special favorably treatment. Seventy-seven percent of students in

33

TABLE 4.10

| | College (by percent) | |
| | More | Less |
Type of Discrimination	Selective	Selective
Faculty	40	43
Overt	2	14
Subtle	29	19

less selective colleges (versus 59 percent in more selective colleges) report that they receive no special favorable treatment. One reason for this difference is the fact that 30 percent at more selective colleges and 43 percent at less selective colleges report little or no contact with faculty members outside class.

Differences in background and treatment such as those described here suggest the likelihood of differences in academic performance, behavior, and reactions to college, and those differences are present. Thirty-six percent of respondents in more selective colleges (versus 23 percent in less selective colleges) report averages of "B" or better. Estimated attrition rates are lower in more selective colleges: 51 percent estimate that less than 10 percent of black students leave, while in less selective colleges only 38 percent estimate attrition rates under 10 percent.

While more students in more selective colleges (60 percent versus 47 percent) feel they were special admits, fewer feel that this has had a negative impact (23 percent versus 42 percent). Related to this is the fact that while the same number of students in more selective and less selective colleges feel there is intense academic competition at their college, fewer at more selective colleges (47 percent versus 66 percent) feel that it has had an impact on them personally.

Major fields are more diverse in more selective colleges, with fewer students (6 percent versus 18 percent) in education, more (9 percent versus 5 percent) in biological sciences, and more (10 percent versus 2 percent) in engineering and math. The desire to attend graduate school also is more widespread in more selective colleges (64 percent) than in less selective colleges (52 percent). In addition, 61 percent of those in more selective colleges (versus 75 percent in less selective colleges) report that their post-graduate plans have not been changed by their college experience.

Reactions of black students to more selective and less selective colleges are different in a number of ways. Fewer students in more selective colleges (32 percent versus 37 percent in less selective colleges) are dissatisfied with their overall experience. The desire for more financial aid (49 percent versus 39 percent) and more recruitment of blacks (62 percent versus 58 percent) is higher in more selective colleges. This results from the fact that more selective colleges tend to be more expensive and to have lower percentages of black enrollment. On the other hand, students in more selective colleges are less concerned about expanding Black Studies programs (20 percent versus 34 percent) and increasing the number of black activities on campus (10 percent versus 15 percent). This results from the fact that more selective colleges tend to have more courses and activities of interest to blacks.

Black students in more selective colleges tend to participate more in all extracurricular activities. Only 19 percent in more selective colleges (versus 27 percent in less selective colleges) report that they participate in no activities. This is true of participation in black organizations (54 percent versus 45 percent) as well as mixed clubs. (Twenty-four percent versus 20 percent) and student government (13 percent versus 10 percent). It does not appear appropriate to attach significance to greater involvement with black organizations as an indicator of greater separatist tendencies because fewer students in more selective colleges (10 percent versus 15 percent) prefer all-black housing.

Finally, it should be noted that black students in more and less selective colleges are virtually identical in several areas. Those areas include their views of whether the college cares about having black students and whether black students as a group can influence programs of the college that affect them. They also include worries about being able to meet the costs of college and belief that colleges should supply more tutoring and remediation to those who need it.

REGION

Grouping predominantly white colleges by geographic region reveals more about the experience of black students in them than grouping those colleges according to any other characteristic. There is so much variation from region to region that three detailed tables are included here for careful examination (see Tables 4.11—4.13). Much of the information about regional differences is surprising. For example, the South has the largest percentage of somewhat satisfied and very satisfied students (73 percent); and the West, the smallest (53 percent). This is in spite of the fact that region is listed as a positive characteristic by more students in the West (52 percent) than in any other region and by fewer in the South (28 percent). While

TABLE 4.11

	Nat'l. Norm	Region			
		NE	MW	S	W
Attend college in home area	78	86	69	83	76
Previously attended another college	25	21	24	18	47
Previously attended two-year public college	49	49	31	33	85
Neither parent attended college	59	66	56	65	42
Applied to only one college	24	16	22	21	52
23 years or older	15	19	10	11	29
Fair/Poor preparation	52	54	55	37	63
Special admit	50	61	45	42	55
Worried about cutbacks	31	41	26	26	30
"C" or better average	85	78	80	93	97
Loan as main source of funds	20	10	24	20	30
Less financial aid available each year	40	35	43	34	54
Positive reaction to region	36	35	37	28	52
Somewhat satisfied or very satisfied	64	58	66	73	53
College doesn't care about black students	67	73	62	58	80
Bitter reaction to college's not caring	18	25	15	14	20
Negative reaction to percentage black enrollment	60	71	53	61	57
Negative reaction to percentage black staff	60	73	50	67	48
Negative reaction to school's responsiveness	61	71	55	54	72
No racial discrimination	51	54	50	56	41
Discrimination from faculty	42	49	35	42	45
Role of inhospitable environment in dropout rate	11	6	7	14	26
Race dominates choice of friends and activities	41	36	40	40	58
Participation in black student organizations	47	52	42	57	34
No participation in activities	25	27	20	20	44
"B" average	25	22	25	23	36
Intense academic competition	59	58	56	55	77
Competition undermines self-confidence	12	11	9	5	26
Plan to attend graduate school	55	57	51	56	58
Don't know rate of attrition	16	19	16	6	31
Positive discrimination	27	29	28	24	23
Negative reaction to positive discrimination	28	42	26	11	28

TABLE 4.12

Major Field	Nat'l. Norm	Region			
		NE	MW	S	W
Social Sciences	28	33	27	25	30
Education	15	26	14	12	3
Business	15	11	13	18	18
Biological Sciences	6	3	6	5	10
Engineering and Math	4	2	3	7	3
Physical Sciences	2	2	2	1	1
English	4	2	5	4	4
Fine Arts	4	4	5	5	4
Black Studies	1	1	-	1	1

TABLE 4.13

Changes	Nat'l. Norm	Region			
		NE	MW	S	W
More recruitment of blacks	59	54	52	78	57
More financial aid, especially for blacks	41	33	43	43	48
Expansion of Black Studies	33	29	28	46	29
More remedial programs and tutoring	24	35	24	10	30
Purge of racists from staff	15	10	14	22	12
More black activities, social life, culture	14	20	10	15	14
More "relevance" in curriculum	5	4	5	3	10
Revised admissions standards	4	4	1	2	12
Greater role in decision making	4	4	4	2	11
Black lounge or center	1	2	-	-	5
All-black housing	1	2	1	-	2

that is paradoxical, it is extremely fortunate. It demonstrates that region, which cannot be changed, is not the problem. Instead, the problem is a series of conditions which prevail at colleges within certain regions and which can be changed.

The West

The problems in the West do not result from the predominance of non-metropolitan colleges (which is not the case), large colleges (which is the case, but which is not associated with the observed differences), or high black enrollment colleges (which is not the case). The problems also are not the result of a predominance of first-generation students because the West has the fewest students from families in which neither parent attended college. In fact, no one characteristic of colleges or students appears to explain variation from region to region.

A combination of several factors which are most evident in the West (and quite apparent in the Northeast, which rivals the West in dissatisfaction) appears to be central to an explanation of regional variation. A majority of students in the West (52 percent) applied to only one college when they were seeking admission to their current college. That is more than twice as many as in any other region. In addition, the West is the only region where the most frequent reason for choosing a particular college was its proximity to the student's home.

Almost twice as many students in the West (47 percent) as in any other region previously attended another college. In the overwhelming majority of cases (85 percent), the previous college was a community college. Students in the West also are slightly more often bothered by fair or poor preparation and are second to the Northeast in percentage of special admits.

Analysis of preparation problems reveals interesting distinctions among students in different regions of the country. Tables 4.14—4.16 indicate the regional distribution of weaknesses in preparation and give more detail about problems of students in the West and the Northeast. Students in the West are much more concerned about weaknesses in science and slightly more concerned about weaknesses in math than any other group.

It should be noted that students in the Northeast probably suffer from similar problems more than the first two lines of Table 4.14 indicate because they are highest in concern about weakness in all areas. In addition, weaknesses of students in the Northeast in math and science appear to be buffered in two ways. First, almost three times as many students in the Northeast as in any other region receive

38

TABLE 4.14

Areas of Inadequate Preparation
for College-Level Work

	Nat'l. Norm	Region			
		NE	MW	S	W
Math	49	36	49	58	65
Science	37	28	38	31	54
English	34	31	27	44	44
All areas	17	26	17	7	16

TABLE 4.15

Valuable Pre-College Experiences
Outside the Classroom

	Nat'l. Norm	Region			
		NE	MW	S	W
Unassigned reading; independent study	46	41	43	58	37
Tutoring or study help by teachers	13	5	19	17	5
Tutoring or study help by others	13	13	16	9	16
Pre-enrollment preparation by college	14	27	10	10	6

TABLE 4.16

Changes Desired for Pre-College Preparation

	Nat'l. Norm	Region			
		NE	MW	S	W
More emphasis on basic skills: spelling, vocabulary or arithmetic	56	59	52	56	64
Learning to read more rapidly	51	53	46	49	60
Learning to express ideas better in writing and/or speaking	46	43	47	42	56
Acquiring more self-discipline; allocate time better	44	43	44	36	59
Acquiring more self-confidence	29	26	29	26	41

special pre-enrollment preparation from their colleges (see Table 4.15). Second, the Northeast has the smallest percentage of students majoring in science and business (see Table 4.12), where preparation in science and math obviously is crucially important.

The general pattern of similarity between the West and Northeast is, however, apparent in most of Tables 4.15 and 4.16. Those regions have the fewest students who received tutoring or study help from teachers at lower levels. They also have the fewest students who were able to use unassigned reading profitably. The West and Northeast also have more students who, if they could redo their preparation for college, would emphasize basic skills, reading rapidly, and self-discipline.

Eighty percent of students in the West—more than in any other region—feel that their college does not care about having black students. Seventy-two percent (a virtual tie with the Northeast) criticize their college's lack of responsiveness. Much, but not all, of the problem in this area is associated with money. More than in any other region, students in the West rely primarily on loans. They also feel, more than students in any other region, that there is less aid available to them each year.

Both the apparent shortage of financial aid funds and the need for them are increased by the fact that colleges in the West have black enrollments which are skewed toward students with low family incomes. As Table 4.17 (and Table 3.1) indicate, the normal pattern for blacks and all students is that the under $5,000 income category is approximately half as well represented in colleges as in the general population. In the West, however, that group is almost as well represented in colleges as in the general population. Less well represented in the West is the $5,000-9,999 category. In addition, the $15,000 and over category is less well represented in the West and the Northeast than in the other regions.

Students in the West find the general college environment less receptive to them. Almost twice as many as in any other region indicate that inhospitable environment contributes to the likelihood that they will drop out. Fewer students in the West (41 percent) than in any other region have not been victims of racial discrimination. More of them (77 percent) perceive intense academic competition, and one-quarter of them feel that it undermines their self-confidence. This is more than twice as many students as in any other region who are unable to deal effectively with competition. The idea that self-confidence is a problem for students in the West is reinforced by Table 4.16. Significantly more students in the West than in any other region would work on increasing their self-confidence if they could prepare again.

40

TABLE 4.17

	$0-4,999	$5,000-9,999	Income $10,000-14,999	$15,000 and over
National Norm				
College Pop.	18	36	25	19
General Pop.	38	34	17	11
NE				
College Pop.	13	38	31	15
General Pop.	31	32	23	14
MW				
College Pop.	17	35	24	24
General Pop.	30	36	20	14
South				
College Pop.	26	38	20	14
General Pop.	46	34	13	7
West				
College Pop.	22	29	29	17
General Pop.	24	38	22	16

Source of general population figures: U.S. Bureau of the Census, 1970.

41

Because preparation is not dramatically different from that in other regions, this reaction to competition suggests severe problems with counseling and other supportive services. Another symptom of the same problem may be the lack of interest in education as a major. Only 3 percent of students in the West are majoring in education even though a more typical problem is overconcentration of blacks in that field. Is this the result of overreaction to stories about an oversupply of teachers unhindered or encouraged by counselors?

In listing changes which they feel would be most beneficial, students in the West reflect the problems they are having. They are first in emphasizing the need for more financial aid. Only students in the Northeast are more interested in increased academic support than those in the West. Almost three times as many students in the West as in any other region want more involvement of blacks in decision making at their college. There also is marked interest in the West in "increased recruitment of black faculty members, administrators, and students."

In spite of this interest, students in the West are less concerned than those in other regions about increasing the percentage of black faculty members and administrators at their college. This is true even though there are proportionately fewer blacks in such positions in the West than in any other region (see Table 4.18). That situation may change, however, as it did in the Northeast after relatively large numbers of students were enrolled for several years.

TABLE 4.18

Staff Members' Estimates of Ratio of
Black Faculty/Administrators to Black Students

| | Nat'l. Norm | Region | | | |
		NE	MW	S	W
1 to 24 or less	24	47	18	9	24
1 to 25—49	40	40	46	48	10
1 to 50 or more	34	9	33	44	66

Table 4.19 indicates a national pattern of increasing black staff in the last two years. In many cases student agitation has helped precipitate increased hiring. Colleges in the West have an opportunity to increase hiring before the pressure mounts.

TABLE 4.19

| Tenure | Staff Members | |
	Black	White
2 years or less	53	19
3—4 years	32	21
5 years or more	15	59

The Northeast

The Northeast is similar to the West in having a low percentage of somewhat and very satisfied black students. It also is similar in many, but not all, of the factors that contribute to satisfaction or dissatisfaction. Some of the similarities already have been mentioned but should be reemphasized. Colleges in both regions tend to have high black enrollment. They have more poorly prepared, special admit students than colleges in other regions. It may, therefore, appear paradoxical that they also are most strongly criticized for being unresponsive to the needs of blacks and for not caring about blacks.

Three other similarities between the Northeast and West exist but have not been mentioned. Because so many students in the Northeast and West are special admits, they are most concerned about cutbacks in special programs for blacks and are afraid that such cutbacks will eliminate their ability to pay for their education. Students in these regions are first and second in saying that their reaction to their college's not caring is "bitterness, disillusionment, etc." Perhaps the amount of rhetoric about colleges being liberal and concerned about equal opportunity is greater in the Northeast and West. In any case, more black students in those regions expect their college to care about them. Finally, students in the Northeast and West also are first and second in identifying the faculty as a source of discrimination.

In spite of the many similarities, significant differences do exist between colleges in the Northeast and West, with many of these differences suggesting more problems for students in the West. A large number of colleges in the West are large, while colleges in the Northeast are more evenly distributed according to size. Western colleges are likely to have few black faculty members and administrators, but colleges in the Northeast are likely to have relatively large numbers of black staff members. Students in the West are second most likely, and students in the Northeast least likely, to be attending college outside their home area. Applying to only one college is typical in the West and quite atypical in the Northeast. Students in the West are most likely, and those in the Northeast least likely, to find that their college has an "inhospitable environment." Finally, in the critical area of financial aid students in the West are most likely, and those in the Northeast least likely, to be primarily dependent on loans and worried about decreasing amounts of aid each year.

Three of the differences between the Northeast and the West, on the other hand, suggest more problems for students in the Northeast. The Northeast has the most first-generation students, and the West the fewest. The Northeast has the largest gap between the academic performance of its black students and their aspirations to attend graduate school. The Northeast is tied for first (57 percent) in students who want to go to graduate school but is tied for last (23 percent) in students with "B" or "A" averages. Finally, the Northeast has the largest percentage of students (29 percent) who feel they receive special favorable treatment and the largest percentage (42 percent) of that group who react negatively to such treatment.

Those numbers and the comments of students both suggest that "positive discrimination" often contains unacceptable and irritating elements of racism expressed as condescension and lower expectations of blacks. Among the comments about special favorable treatment are:

> I felt as if I were set aside, not special, and I had to capitalize on my being black. I wrote papers on being black and received very good grades despite deficient English. I felt like an unoffending pet.

> It gives a hollow sense of power.

The Midwest

The Midwest is in the middle in many ways. It exhibits characteristics most strongly or least strongly in only a few cases, but it is first in satisfaction among the three regions containing colleges with high black enrollment. It also is tied with the South in being perceived as most responsive to the needs of blacks. The characteristics which are most evident in the Midwest, therefore, deserve considerable attention. Midwestern colleges are tied for first place in enrolling the largest numbers of black students. They are second in the percentage of black faculty members and administrators employed. Increasing the number of black staff members along with the number of black students appears to have been important. The importance of this step is increased because the Midwest has the largest percentage of black students from other regions, and those students tend to have special problems adjusting to college.

Several other factors may contribute to the high level of satisfaction in the Midwest. It is first in students with family incomes over $15,000 (24 percent, versus 17 percent in the West, 15 percent in the Northeast, and 14 percent in the South). There are fewer students who previously attended a community college in the Midwest than in any other region. The Midwest is third in special admits and last in worry about cutbacks in special programs. Fewer students in the Midwest than in any other region feel they have been discriminated against by faculty members. The Midwest is virtually tied with the Northeast in terms of students receiving special treatment. The nature of that "positive discrimination" appears to be different in the Midwest, however, because midwestern students are much lower in negative reaction to it than those in the Northeast. Finally, the Midwest has the second smallest gap between the percentage of black students with "B" averages or better and the percentage planning to go to graduate school.

The South

The South, which is first in the percentage of black students who are satisfied with their college experience, is distinctive in several critical ways. Probably the most surprising, and perhaps the most important, distinctive characteristic is the relatively low level of racial discrimination in southern colleges. As Table 4.11 indicates, the South has the largest group (56 percent) who have experienced no racial discrimination at college. The same table indicates that only the Midwest has fewer problems in the critical area of discrimination by faculty members. Not coincidentally, faculty members in the South and the Midwest are perceived to be much more accessible to black students than in the Northeast or West. Thirty-seven percent of students in the South and 34 percent in the Midwest find accessibility of faculty to be a positive characteristic of their colleges. The corresponding figures for the Northeast and West are 29 percent and 22 percent. In addition, fewer black students in the South (13 percent) than in any other region (Midwest, 17 percent; Northeast, 27 percent; and West, 31 percent) feel they have been subjected to subtle forms of discrimination which can be the hardest types to counter.

There are no colleges in the South with high black enrollment. There also are fewer students in the South than in any other region who are poorly prepared or who are special admits. Finally, there are fewer students in the South than in any other region who feel that their college does not care about black students or who worry about cutbacks in special programs.

It must be emphasized here that this data is in no way an argument for ignoring the disadvantaged. If anything, it supports the opposite conclusion. The South does, after all, have the largest percentage of first-generation students and the largest percentage of students whose family incomes are under $5,000.

The unique characteristic of colleges in the South is that their black students are not markedly different academically from their white students. Black students in the South more than in any other region feel they are as well prepared and as competent as white students. Fewer students in the South than in any other region feel that their preparation was weak in all areas or weak in science. Similarly, fewer students in the South are concerned about their self-discipline or self-confidence. In addition, students in the South are more certain that their fellow students will complete their education. Table 4.20 gives detailed information on students' views of attrition rates for black students.

TABLE 4.20

Attrition Rate (estimated)	Nat'l. Norm	Region			
		NE	MW	S	W
Up to 24 percent	56	47	52	80	47
25 percent or more	23	33	30	10	14
Don't know	16	19	16	6	31

Staff members in the South agree with black students there. Far fewer staff members in the South than in any other region feel that preparation of black students is fair or poor or that the overall academic performance of black students is worse than that of whites (see Table 5.2 in Chapter 5).

This apparently helps blacks in the South to avoid being perceived as a different and monolithic group with only limited interests and abilities. Staff members in the South feel much less than those in other regions that black students are different from whites. Staff members in the South also feel much less than those in other regions that blacks concentrate in certain major fields of study. There is, in fact, more diversity in the majors of black students in the South than in any other region. Perhaps this results partially from the fact that less astonishment is generated among staff members in the South when black students appear somewhere besides in social sciences and education.

It should be noted that colleges in the South have fewer black staff members than any other region except the West. This probably causes fewer problems in the South than it would elsewhere for two reasons. First, the South has by far the highest black population of any region, so role models and sources of advice in addition to those at colleges are available to black students. Second, whites in the South may be more adept at relating openly to blacks partly because blacks in the South do have alternatives to dealing with them. Nevertheless, increasing black staff is perceived as a significant need by both students and staff members in this region.

Colleges in the South also are distinctive in terms of jobs held by black students and the reaction of the students to their work. In the South more working students (67 percent) than in any other region (Northeast, 41 percent; Midwest, 59 percent; and West, 43 percent) have jobs on campus (see Table 4.21).

TABLE 4.21

Location of Job(s)	Nat'l. Norm	Region			
		NE	MW	S	W
On campus	53	41	59	67	43
Both on and off campus	10	16	7	8	7
Off campus	35	39	33	24	51

Fewer students in the South (12 percent) than in any other region (Northeast, 31 percent; Midwest, 39 percent; and West, 52 percent) feel their work affects them negatively. It is interesting to note that the incidence of off-campus jobs and negative reaction to work are identical in the West. When more information can be gathered about the nature of the work done and the rate of compensation, it should be possible to assess more accurately the importance of the location and amount of time of jobs.

Fortunately, most of the distinctive positive characteristics of colleges in the South are not exclusively the result of its peculiar history. They can be reproduced in any of the other regions through alterations in the way black students are perceived, recruited, and treated.

NOTES

1. See Charles V. Willie and Arline Sakuma McCord, Black Students at White Colleges (New York: Praeger Publishers, 1972).

2. The typology established by James Cass and Max Birnbaum in Comparative Guide to American Colleges: 1970-1971 is widely used and has been adopted here. "More selective" here includes the following Cass and Birnbaum categories: "very selective," "highly selective," and "most selective."

5

DIFFERENCES IN
PERCEPTIONS BETWEEN
STAFF MEMBERS
AND BLACK STUDENTS

Is the way black students see their college experience the way
it really is? Probably not completely, but to work with them effectively, one needs to know their views. Similarly, faculty members
and administrators at predominantly white colleges may not see those
colleges and the black students in them as they really are, but it is
important to know the views of these staff members. Staff and students
agree about many, but not all, problems of black students in predominantly white colleges. In cases in which the viewpoints of students
and staff are dissimilar, it is unlikely that problems will be solved
until perspectives of either or both groups can be changed. In cases
in which the viewpoints are similar, the foundations for problem
solving exist. The task of building something on them, however, re-
mains.

The perceptions of faculty members and administrators are
similar to those of black students in areas such as class attendance
of blacks and characteristics of colleges which have negative impact.
They differ dramatically, however, about the overall reaction of blacks
to their college experience. Two-thirds of the black students are
somewhat or very satisfied, but college staff members feel that only
one-third are somewhat or very satisfied.

The pessimism of the staff appears to relate to their feelings
about the preparation, academic experience, and finances of black
students. Staff members are substantially less impressed with the
preparation of black students than students are. Seventy-three percent
of the staff, but only 52 percent of the students, evaluate the preparation of black students as fair or poor. In spite of this, only 31 percent of staff members feel the preparation of black students is so bad
that it suggests that less demanding admissions standards are being
applied to blacks. The staff also is less convinced than students that
blacks participate fully in class or have good study habits. Sixty-one

percent of the staff and 81 percent of the students think the classroom participation of blacks is as good as that of whites. Forty-six percent of the staff, versus 72 percent of the students, feel that black students' study habits are as good as those of whites. Finally, 64 percent of staff members, compared to 47 percent of students, emphasize students' insecurity about finances.

Although both academic and financial factors are emphasized by staff members, they are more concerned about academic factors. The list of changes which staff members think would benefit black students is similar to the list provided by students, but greater emphasis is placed on efforts to remedy academic deficiencies. Table 5.1 indicates the priorities assigned by faculty members.

Observations about staff members as a group such as those presented so far are enlightening. To understand fully the experience of black students, however, it is necessary to examine subgroups of staff. Breaking staff into smaller groups sometimes is unproductive, but often it reveals additional information. The three subgroups which provide greatest insight are based on position (faculty member or administrator), race, and region of employment.

POSITION

There is no particular difference between the views of faculty members and administrators on many topics. Neither faculty members (41 percent) nor administrators (47 percent) are as concerned as black students (61 percent) about increasing their college's responsiveness to the needs of blacks. Neither group attributes much importance to the role of students' families in problem solving. Students disagree and list family more often than any other source of help for both financial and personal problems. Neither staff group rates white

TABLE 5.1

Changes	Percentage Staff
More supportive services, remediation	27
More recruitment of black students and staff	15
More financial aid	12
Expansion of Black Studies	11
Curriculum changes to reflect relevance	9
In-service training for faculty	8

administrators as highly as black students do in terms of the contribution of white administrators to problem solving.

On some topics, however, the views of faculty members and administrators are quite different. In comparison to faculty members (and students), administrators overrate the role of black administrators as sources of help for black students. Faculty members, on the other hand, overrate black faculty members as sources of help. Administrators are more pessimistic than faculty members about the academic experience of black students. Perhaps this occurs because faculty members see a representative sample of students, while administrators see primarily students who are having problems.

In any case, faculty members' perception of the academic experience of black students is closer to the students' own perception of their experience. Preparation of black students is fair or poor according to 52 percent of students, 69 percent of faculty members, and 81 percent of administrators. Class participation of blacks is at least as good as that of whites according to more than 80 percent of black students and 78 percent of faculty members but only 39 percent of administrators. Study habits of blacks are comparable to those of whites according to 72 percent of students, 52 percent of faculty members, and 36 percent of administrators.

RACE

Black and white staff members watch black students from different vantage points. More often than not they disagree about what they see. At the most general level of evaluation, 46 percent of whites, but only 29 percent of blacks, feel that black students are somewhat or very satisfied. On the subject of overall satisfaction, therefore, whites' perceptions are closer to the experience of black students than those of black staff members are. This could be the result of the often alleged search for "militants" to take staff positions at white colleges. It also could result from the tendency of black students to be more inclined to discuss freely, or even exaggerate, their problems when talking with black staff members. In fact, both factors could be at work. More academically oriented (sometimes known as less militant) staff members are less likely to accept at face value assertions that all of a student's problems stem from racism. These staff members may, therefore, hear fewer sweeping complaints about their colleges.

In general, black staff members are more critical of colleges and high schools than whites are. White staff members, in turn, are more critical of black students. Opinions differ most about what colleges are doing for black students. Seventy-seven percent of black

51

staff members, 65 percent of whites, and 52 percent of black students feel that black students have received fair or poor preparation. More than twice as many black staff members (53 percent) as whites (24 percent) feel that colleges are not responsive enough to the needs of black students. Sixty-one percent of black students share that opinion.

Although neither group strongly advocates this, three times as many black staff members (10 percent) as whites (3 percent) feel that there should be in-service training for faculty members to improve their relationships with black students. More than three times as many blacks (49 percent) as whites (14 percent) feel that faculty members are not as accessible as they should be to black students. Forty-two percent of black students share that opinion. Finally, very few staff members feel there is no racial discrimination at their college, but more than four times as many of those who see no discrimination are whites (22 percent) as blacks (5 percent).

The difference between the opinions of black and white staff members on three other topics indicates problems in the relationship between black students and white staff members. More white (43 percent) than black (30 percent) staff members feel that the overall academic performance of black students is worse than that of whites. Similarly, more white (83 percent) than black (53 percent) staff members feel that less demanding admissions standards for blacks are a good idea. Despite these feelings about academic deficiencies of blacks, fewer white (63 percent) than black (79 percent) staff members are making special efforts to help black students. In other words, more white than black staff members feel that black students have academic problems, but whites do less than blacks to help these students perform adequately.

The data presented here suggest two good reasons for employing substantial numbers of black faculty members. First, their opinions can somewhat counterbalance those of whites who are insensitive to certain problems of black students. Second, their opinions will be less likely to result in oversimplification of problems if several perspectives are present within the group of black staff members.

REGION

Looking at staff members in regional groups confirms several earlier observations. The West is the region with fewest black staff members (with the Northeast first, the Midwest second, and the South third) and the highest percentage (95 percent) of staff who feel that black students are different. As the last section indicates it should be, the West also is the region where there is greatest divergence between the views of staff and those of students. In addition, the gap between staff and student views is biggest on the subject of deficiencies of colleges, just as the last section suggests it would be. Even though the views of staff members differ considerably from region to region, in most cases they are parallel to those of students. Within regions, staff and students agree much more often than they disagree.

Examining the rank order of staff and student responses by region is the best way of determining the extent to which they agree. Rank orders for satisfaction provide a good example. Staff members see the distribution of somewhat and very satisfied students as follows: the South and Midwest tied for first, the Northeast third, and the West fourth (see Table 5.2). Students vary only in that the Midwest is second rather than tied for first. Similarity between staff and student views within regions exists even on sensitive topics like lack of responsiveness of colleges and inaccessibility of faculty members as negative characteristics. Both groups feel that the West exhibits the negative traits most.

Colleges in the West do not, however, appear ready to solve these problems about which a consensus exists. The reason is that two of the changes students want most are wanted least by staff members. Students in the West are first in desire for more financial aid, with 48 percent listing it as an important change. Only 2 percent of staff members in the West share this view. Students in the West are second only to those in the Northeast in wanting more academic support services (remediation, tutoring, or counseling). Staff members in the West give least support of those in any region to this type of change, with only 8 percent favoring increases.

There are two areas where colleges in the West may be ready to move towards improving the experience of black students. Both staff and students place relatively great emphasis on the need for more black staff members. In addition, more staff members in the West than in any other region advocate in-service training for faculty as a means of improving their relationships with black students. Progress in these areas would make a difference to black students in the West. It also should make it easier to institute change in financial aid and academic assistance by increasing the staff's perception of problems in these areas.

One of the areas in which staff and students in the West disagree is the only area of major disagreement in the Northeast. Roles are reversed in the Northeast, however, with staff members being more enthusiastic advocates than students are of increases in financial aid. While staff members in the Northeast are first in proposing increases in financial aid, students in the Northeast are last in proposing that change.

The situation in the Midwest is similar. Staff members are more concerned than students about two problems. Staff members

TABLE 5.2

Staff Members' Views	Nat'l. Norm	Region			
		NE	MW	S	W
On Black Students:					
Students somewhat or very satisfied	36	21	48	48	15
Class attendance as good as whites'	72	61	69	87	75
Class participation as good as whites'	61	58	58	76	53
Study habits as good as whites'	46	31	36	71	57
Overall academic performance worse than whites'	34	51	33	15	39
Fair or poor academic preparation	73	94	74	46	84
Negative reaction of black students to percentage black enrollment	58	64	56	51	68
Negative reaction of black students to percentage black faculty members and administrators	57	68	51	55	55
Negative reaction of black students to college's lack of responsiveness	43	42	40	26	87
Negative reaction of black students to inaccessibility of faculty	37	33	34	31	65
No racial discrimination at school	20	20	13	29	21
Less demanding admissions standards applied to black students	31	48	24	19	37
Less demanding standards a good idea	60	60	53	86	48
Gives special treatment to black students	73	73	85	58	71
Black students expect special treatment	7	6	6	10	8
Black students different from white students	59	55	64	37	95
On Desirable Changes:					
More recruitment of black students and staff	15	6	11	30	18
More financial aid	12	19	12	12	2
Expansion of Black Studies	8	6	6	14	6
More remedial programs and tutoring	15	21	15	13	3
More counseling and supportive services	12	8	22	6	5
In-service training for faculty	8	5	3	13	16

54

are second in identifying inaccessibility of faculty as a problem, but students in the Midwest are less concerned about it than those in any other region. In addition, staff members in the Midwest are first in wanting to increase academic support services, but students are only third in advocating that change.

The South, because of its peculiar history, has the unusual combination of fewest black staff members and least divergence between the opinions of staff and students. The South is last in percentage of staff (37 percent) who feel that blacks are different. It also has only one significant difference between the views of staff and students. Staff members in the South give less emphasis than those in any other region to low black enrollment as a negative characteristic of their schools. Students in the South, however, are second only to those in the Northeast in emphasizing that negative characteristic. In spite of this difference, both staff and students in the South are first in advocating increased black recruitment as an important change.

CHAPTER

6

IMPLICATIONS AND
RECOMMENDATIONS

It seems clear that so much new data, analyzed fairly, compels
certain inferences and uncovers new insights which are basically
positive in tone. In spite of predictions of large-scale disasters
for the academic standards of colleges and the development of individual black students, attempts to move beyond token desegregation
appear to be succeeding. Significant, although insufficient, progress
toward equal opportunity has been made in the first four years of
effort.

Fortunately, the data assembled here does not corroborate all
the pessimistic conclusions quoted in Chapter 1. The experience of
most black students in predominantly white colleges, for example,
does not appear to be blighted by admissions practices which favor
"less qualified black students who fit a . . . fashionable stereotype."
Such a conclusion may represent a valid observation about a few
colleges, but it does not reflect the situation at all colleges across
the country.

Perhaps colleges have sought to do the right thing by stimulating
the diversity which should exist within black student populations.
Whether they have done this, have been lucky, or simply have failed
in their attempts to screen out diversity, most black student contin-
gents are not monolithic. On the other hand, in the few cases where
it is appropriate to talk about a basically monolithic black student
population, the academic, personal, and social results are bad (see
Chapter 2).[1]

Although there are colleges where race relations are extremely
strained, it is not true in most colleges that a "near total segregation
in all but classroom activities" prevails. In assessing the segregation which persists, it must be remembered that much of it is neither
new nor the result of an ideology of separatism. It is, rather, reflec-
tive of social conditions in the country and the general population.

College groups often divide along racial lines because both whites and blacks have been socialized to be comfortable with that kind of division. A variation on that theme according to several respondents involves the feeling among both whites and blacks that friendships across racial lines are a kind of "kid stuff" which works in high school but falls apart in college. Ideological separatism is not new, and it is the rallying cry of only a minority of black students.

This is true although a majority of black students agree with the charge that predominantly white colleges are "unprepared (and in many cases unwilling to be prepared) to meet their needs." The response of these students is not to write off the institutions as hopeless, but to try to meet many of their own needs themselves while trying to change the colleges. As a result, black students can criticize the lack of responsiveness of colleges while being satisfied with the overall college experience. There is no more of a "back to Africa" movement on white college campuses than there is in the society as a whole.* There is, on the contrary, a determination to alter those campuses in ways which make them comfortable as well as beneficial for all students.

Even now, when discrimination, being stereotyped as special admits, and other problems distract black students,[2] they are able to concentrate well enough to obtain college educations and degrees. In fact, most of them want to go on to graduate school even though it is likely that they will have to run the same kind of obstacle course there. Black students want and deserve the opportunity to enroll anywhere their talents and interests lead them.

The overall pattern of success should not be surprising. After all, most black students are within accepted admissions parameters for the college where they are enrolled. This is true in spite of demeaning rhetoric that any black can get into any college in the country even though few are qualified. Another bit of demeaning and damaging rhetoric holds that blacks seek and get a free ride through college. The data here about loans and jobs shows that few black students are getting a free ride (unless it is provided by their own families). The data also shows that college education is something that most blacks take seriously enough to work to overcome gaps in their preparation.

Colleges, however, have not yet made it clear that they are willing to work hard to overcome gaps in their preparation for dealing

---

*In both this survey and a nationwide survey of black adults conducted in February-March 1972 for Ebony magazine by Daniel Yankelovich, Inc., only a small minority of the respondents could legitimately be called "separatists."

with black students. In fact, data about changes which staff members feel are desirable (see Table 5.2) suggests that their complacency is as much a problem as disagreement with students about what changes are needed. To develop and/or demonstrate willingness to work, colleges can do many things including establishing formal in-service training for staff members.

When deciding whether to consider in-service training, college policy makers should think about at least two things. First, such training was suggested by a significant number of respondents in this study. Second, four years may be long enough to try muddling through an important transitional period, sometimes without so much as a comprehensive, faculty meeting discussion. In charting a course for the next four years, formalized issue raising and answer seeking might be productive. It might even be critical.

An example of a step colleges need to take, and of the limits to muddling through, is affirmative action for staff positions. Currently, many colleges are engaged in special efforts to recruit, retain, and advance black staff members. Few of them, however, appear to understand that these efforts are necessary for educational as well as legal, moral, and symbolic reasons. As such, affirmative action should be a mainstream activity of colleges rather than merely a backwater ritual designed to appease rather than satisfy blacks, government agencies, and other constituencies. Affirmative action then, like other mainstream activities, should be evaluated according to its results rather than just the complexity of its procedures. To paraphrase a well known feminist, a mediocre black person should have as much chance to move into and up organizations as the mediocre whites who now fill so many positions at all levels. Moreover, outstanding blacks should be able to dislodge the barnacle-tight grip of mediocre whites who were able to attach themselves originally only because blacks were considered to be ineligible. In other words, outstanding blacks should not be restricted to competing for recently created "black" jobs.

All students will receive better educations when blacks are represented in all major areas of college life and at all levels within those areas. That kind of representation will signal the success of affirmative action. Having more blacks than before in "black" jobs at lower and middle levels will not entitle colleges to claim success in affirmative action or to reap the educational benefits of real success.

As progress is made on affirmative action it will become easier to make progress in institutionalizing exchange about the education of black students among and between faculty members and administrators, particularly between blacks and whites. This hopefully would make it possible for staff members to deal with each

58

black student individually without prejudging the student's background, ability, or interests. At a minimum, it would enable more staff members to deal with black students on the basis of facts and reasonable assumptions rather than wild guesses about them. Until reliable feedback channels can be opened from black students to all staff members, exchanges of information among staff members will be crucial.

It also is crucial to remember that the possible actions suggested above and the recommendations which follow are not options for rich colleges only. Much of what troubles black students in predominantly white colleges did not develop because the colleges were short of money. It also cannot be eliminated merely by spending money. Anyone who thinks everything that can be done to increase equality of opportunity costs a lot of money simply is wrong.

In addition, anyone who thinks expenditures for equal opportunity are nothing more than charitable contributions should consider the return to colleges on an investment in equal opportunity for black students. That return can take a number of forms in addition to helping whites reach accord with their consciences. One form of return involves the ability of the college to be "relevant." Calls for relevance from students of all colors have involved not just linkage to the world of work but also linkage to other parts of the "real world." Having blacks on campus and in the curriculum increases ability to supply this kind of relevance. Another form of return involves the ability of a college to respond to external as well as internal pressure for black employment and advancement while maintaining appropriate standards for staff members. Recruiting and retaining black professionals on a par with white professionals at a given college is much easier when that college has a large, diverse, and reasonably well satisfied black student population.

The greatest return on an investment in equal opportunity is the result of a tendency for black students to provide insight into ways of dealing with problems for all students. A major example of this involves advising and counseling. The constant requests of black students and their advocates for more and better advising and counseling usually is perceived as, at best, an appropriate response to the needs of the disadvantaged. As the reliance on required courses and prerequisites for courses decreases, however, an increasing number of students of all races find the advising and counseling system inadequate. The majority of students and their parents may be slow to demand changes in the system because they know it always has been that way. Blacks, who do not know or do not care how it always was, have demanded and will continue to demand changes which ultimately can benefit the entire institution.

A related example of the way blacks can highlight problems and perhaps speed the process of solving them involves accessibility of faculty members. While many white students accept lack of access to professors outside the classroom as part of the game, black students complain bitterly about it. In fact, many of the charges of discrimination by faculty members involve outside contact. In some cases, students cite evidence that professors are available to white, but not black, students. More importantly, black students find it easy to believe, without specific evidence, that they must be victims of discrimination. When they are unable to get any of a professor's time, they naturally assume that it is going to someone else. It is incomprehensible to them that teachers may show equal lack of interest in all their students or that the system encourages this lack of interest. This kind of "naivete" can be refreshing and beneficial as institutions try to upgrade the quality of their learning environments.

It also should be remembered that there are costs involved in trying to stop or reverse the momentum toward equal opportunity which has been developed just as there are costs in going ahead. The decline in demonstrations by black students in the past three years appears to be based on a balance between satisfaction with the gains that were achieved in 1969-70 and the desire for further improvements. Therefore, if some of these improvements do not develop soon, another era of confrontation could result. It is doubtful that a return to the campus climate of 1969-70 would produce progress. Instead it might end the courtship between white colleges and black students and undermine the progress which has been achieved.

Confrontation is not the only possible consequence of a failure of white colleges to open themselves further to blacks. Other possibilities include a massive shift of black enrollment to traditionally black institutions and/or a return to the status quo ante. If black students feel certain that predominantly white colleges wish to go no farther toward equal opportunity than expanded tokenism, many of them could opt for the more hospitable environment of black colleges. Predominantly white colleges could make the decision to go elsewhere almost certain by providing little financial aid, few supportive services, almost no black staff, and heavy doses of racial discrimination. From a practical viewpoint this would produce great pressures on those black colleges—primarily public universities— which attempted to double or triple their enrollments over a short period. From a philosophical viewpoint the ramifications could be enormous. A shift away from inhospitable white colleges would mark the end of the first American experiment in free enterprise with regard to black students and staff in higher education.

A return to the previous monopolistic system at a time when blacks are beginning to be accepted as eligible for any college in the country would be tragic and dangerous. Blacks then would attend black colleges while whites attended white colleges. The only exception would be the case of the elite among black students and faculty who could become the objects of competition and pressure of unprecedented intensity. The most important consequence of this shift would be acceleration of the drift toward two nations—one white and one black—which the Kerner Commission cited.

If black colleges could not obtain sufficient support for the necessary expansion, the result could be a rapid shrinkage in the options available to blacks in higher education. Unfortunately, there is nothing in the historical record to suggest that the necessary financial support would be forthcoming. If black colleges were unable to meet the demand, community colleges and postsecondary training institutions could become the only available educational outlets for the majority of black high school graduates.

A step which colleges need to take beyond cost/benefit analyses is placing a positive value on improving the experience of black students as an end in itself. After taking that step, colleges may find it valuable to compare very satisfied and dissatisfied black students. Such a comparison can provide hints about ways to improve the experience of all black students, and possibly of all students regardless of race. Tables 6.1 and 6.2 contain a great deal of information about factors which contribute to differences in levels of satisfaction among black students.

The factors which affect satisfaction levels are in two categories: characteristics of students and aspects of their experience at college. Because so many factors are acting and interacting, it would be surprising if they produced a high degree of uniformity among those students who are very satisfied and among those who are dissatisfied. They do not. There are, however, a few statements which apply to most (55 percent or more) of the students in each group.

Students who are very satisfied with their overall college experience are almost twice as likely as those who are dissatisfied to have considered the academic reputation of their college when they were making their choice. Very satisfied students also are more confident than dissatisfied students that black students can influence programs which affect them at their college. This obviously means that colleges can influence the relative size of the two groups by encouraging or discouraging black students to: (1) weigh the quality of the academic match between themselves and a given college; and (2) share in college decision making and responsibility.

More characteristics and experiences are shared by a majority of dissatisfied students than by those who are very satisfied. Most dissatisfied students, and almost as many very satisfied students, feel that their preparation was fair or poor. The gap between them

TABLE 6.1

Differences in Characteristics Between Students
Very Satisfied and Those Dissatisfied with their Overall College Experience

Student Characteristics	Nat'l. Norm	Percentage Black Students	
		Very Satisfied	Dissatisfied
Grew up in:			
Large city	56	37	63
Small city	23	32	18
Suburban area	10	21	9
Family Income:			
Less than $5,000	18	16	22
$5,000-9,999	36	40	32
$10,000-14,999	25	32	25
$15,000 and over	19	9	18
Academic preparation for college:			
Fair or poor	52	47	55
Inadequate preparation in:			
Math	49	31	57
Science	37	47	38
English	34	25	31
Overall	17	12	23
Considered academic reputation of college when choosing this school	48	68	37
Admitted under special circumstances based on race ("special admit")	50	41	60
College loan the primary source of financial aid	11	6	17
Race a dominant factor in choice of friends and activities	41	33	56
Maintain "B" average or better	25	24	25
Likely to drop out of this college	23	8	35

TABLE 6.2

Differences in Attitudes Between Students
Very Satisfied and Those Dissatisfied with
their Overall College Experience

Student Attitudes	Nat'l. Norm	Percentage Black Students	
		Very Satisfied	Dis- satisfied
College is unresponsive to needs of blacks	61	52	72
Black students can influence college programs which affect them	57	66	47
Academic competition undermines self-confidence	12	11	21
Impact of "special admit" status on life at college:			
None	59	67	50
Negative:			
Feel like an outsider	16	5	23
Pushed toward a certain major	4	2	15
Victim of discrimination:			
in general	49	30	60
from faculty	42	19	48
More financial aid should be available	41	26	47
Estimated attrition rate of black students:			
25% or more	23	8	33

is larger, however, when various aspects of preparation are high-lighted. Dissatisfied students are substantially more conscious than very satisfied students of weakness in math and in all areas. Probably as a result, dissatisfied students are considerably more likely than very satisfied students to feel they were special admits.

Once they are in college, dissatisfied students continue to share experiences which touch very satisfied students less frequently. Dissatisfied students find that their colleges are unresponsive to the needs of blacks more often than very satisfied students do. More specifically, dissatisfied students are twice as likely to experience racial discrimination and two-and-a-half times as likely to identify faculty members as the source of that discrimination. Not surprisingly, dissatisfied students are much more likely to indicate that race is a dominant factor in their choice of friends and activities.

Dissatisfied students also are much more likely than very satisfied students to focus upon financial concerns and problems with finishing their educations. Almost twice as many dissatisfied as very satisfied students feel more financial aid should be available. Even more striking is the fact that that four times as many dissatisfied as very satisfied students feel that attrition among blacks at their college is more than 25 percent. In addition, dissatisfied students are four times as likely to indicate they may drop out themselves. Some of the reasons for the alienation expressed in the statistics about attrition already have been mentioned. An additional reason which should be considered is the fact that dissatisfied students are much more likely than very satisfied students to feel that being a special admit has a negative effect at their college. Four times as many dissatisfied as very satisfied students say that being a special admit makes one feel like an outsider. More importantly, seven times as many say that special admits are pushed toward certain "black" majors by their colleges.

Finally, it should be noted that almost twice as many dissatisfied as very satisfied students come from large cities. On the other hand, the much smaller group from suburban areas is more than twice as well represented in the very satisfied group as in the dissatisfied group. Interestingly, this dramatic difference cannot be attributed to high family income in the suburbs and low family income in the city. In fact, the group from large cities has greater representation in the $15,000 and up category than in any other category, and the group from the suburbs has lower representation in the top income category than in any other one (see Table 6.3).

Factors which help explain the greater satisfaction of suburban students include both student characteristics and college experiences. Students from suburban areas tend to be better prepared than those from large cities. They also are more likely to be female. Perhaps

TABLE 6.3

| | Home | |
	Large City	Suburban Area
National Norm	56	10
Age		
17-18	50	15
19-20	59	11
21-22	58	5
Sex		
Male	58	8
Female	54	13
Family Income		
0-4,999	52	8
5,000-9,999	57	8
10,000-14,999	52	15
15,000+	66	7
Preparation		
Excellent/Good	50	12
Fair/Poor	63	8
College's Black Enrollment		
Low	49	11
Medium	51	10
High	62	10
Class Year		
1st	54	13
2nd	61	11
3rd	55	8
4th	55	7
Victim of Discrimination		
Yes	60	7
No	53	13
Influence of Race		
Much	63	6
Little	50	12

most important, suburban students are most highly represented among the youngest age group and the first-year group. Students from large cities are least well represented in the same groups. This suggests again the possibility that colleges are becoming more skillful at gaining exposure to and admitting black students. In other words, colleges may not be drawing as heavily on the largest and most obvious, but not necessarily most disadvantaged, concentrations of blacks.

Once students from suburban areas are enrolled, they are less likely to be victims of discrimination than those from large cities. This is explained partly by the fact that students from large cities have greater representation at colleges with high levels of black enrollment where there tends to be more discrimination. It also is explained partly by the relative emphasis on race as a determining factor in choosing friends and activities. Students from large cities are more likely to feel that race has a dominant influence than that it has little influence. Students from suburban areas, however, are more likely to feel that race has little influence than that it has a dominant influence. As a result, students from suburban areas probably blend in more easily and do not stand out as targets for discrimination.

This description of dissatisfied and very satisfied students suggests that colleges who want more of the latter should keep several things in mind. They should emphasize the match between the preparation, ability, interests, and style of each prospective black student and the academic reputation, requirements, and style of the college. They should evaluate and try to reduce the extent of discrimination on campus. They also should beware of the pitfalls of having special admissions programs become the first stage of a "Scarlet Letter" syndrome which plagues students throughout their college careers. This, in turn, is related to the need for colleges to be responsive to the needs of blacks and to the recommendations presented in the remaining section of this chapter.

These recommendations do not represent a simple answer or a set of simple answers to the problems of providing full equality of opportunity in higher education. The problems are much too complex for answers of that type. In fact, the problems are so complex that full solutions to them are as difficult to conceive as they are to implement. The recommendations, therefore, are offered as reference points for those who want to continue the challenging and vitally important process of removing barriers which still face black students in predominantly white colleges.

RECOMMENDATIONS

"Any attempt to produce first-rate education for black
Americans will have to begin by finding out what has
actually been done so far—and with what results. On
most campuses this question has scarcely been asked,
much less answered."[3]

This study asks and answers basic questions about the experience
of blacks at predominantly white colleges. The obvious next step is
for those colleges along with prospective and actual black students
to examine the data carefully and respond to it constructively. To
assist them a summary of conclusions and general recommendations
follows. More specific goals and procedures will have to be developed
for individual colleges according to their particular histories as
well as variations in region, location, and the like.

1. Colleges should attempt to be more responsive to the needs
of blacks.

This is both the most general and the most important recommendation. It requires explanation because it is so general and because many whites feel enough, or too much, has been done for blacks
already. The key is not how much has been done, but what has been
done. The data here clearly indicates that more has been done to
meet the peripheral needs of blacks than to meet their central needs.
No matter how much fanfare accompanies the prevailing type of
"responsiveness," it is not likely to change the conclusion that colleges are unresponsive.

The responses to this survey indicate that for colleges to be
responsive to the needs of black students they must deal with the
needs of black students on three levels of descending priority. The
three levels are related or overlapping in that meeting lower level
needs can either help or hinder efforts to meet those at the crucial
first level. If dealing with lower level needs helps to meet top priority
needs, the effort is extremely valuable. If, however, dealing with
lower level needs hinders meeting top priority needs, the effort is
worthless or even damaging.

The first needs are those which have to be met if a college
experience is to be meaningful as anything more than a way to delay
entry into the job market. The needs are more than marginal economic survival as well as opportunities for intellectual and psychological growth. If pursuit of economic survival is so difficult that
it leaves little physical or mental energy for other activities, there
is a good chance that nothing else can be accomplished. Likewise,
while intellectual growth should be reflected by the maintenance of
a respectable grade point average, it also must include other elements.

67

They are exchange and debate with faculty unfettered by racial stereotyping, full exposure to unfamiliar educational and career options, acquisition of marketable skills, as well as development of analytical and critical faculties. Psychological growth involves increasing readiness to apply the results of intellectual growth in the real world. It is based on confidence in one's individual identity and efforts as decisive factors for much success or failure.

The second set of needs involves major institutional adjustments which indicate to black students and everyone else the transition from an exclusionary and racist system to an open and open-minded system. Substantial numbers of black staff and students as well as a curriculum which reflects awareness of the accomplishments and problems of blacks are called for. Getting started with a sense of direction in these areas is difficult; but once significant momentum has been gained, it is relatively easy to maintain. Colleges must be careful not to mistake extensions of the current system for the necessary changes. Large numbers of staff members, students, and black oriented courses which fit white stereotypes rather than black needs are not the answer.

The need for a sizeable and diverse group of black staff members involves the need for varied role models as black students try to decide whether to try anything other than the most familiar fields. It also involves the need to have people whom black students can trust as they and white staff members seek to develop a basis of mutual trust. Similarly, a large and diverse group of black students provides opportunities for extensive interaction with other blacks without the strains and increasing ghettoization which are typical of small minority groups. Black students then gradually can develop confidence in greater interaction with whites. The need for a revised curriculum arises from the deplorable omissions and distortions which persist in most curriculums.

Third-level needs involve minor institutional adjustments which may signify nothing more than a new tokenism. The needs are special social and political channels which ease the adjustment of black students to important aspects of college life in addition to the academic ones. All-black lounges, centers, or dormitories and special entertainment or cultural budgets and/or events are examples of the social needs. Special recruiting, advising, and counseling or disciplinary channels are examples of the political needs. Most blacks know how to swim in these special channels because they have been in similar situations all their lives. Some of them want and need to have such channels available at college for changes of pace from the difficult task of learning to swim in the mainstream. Many black students want, and all of them deserve, chances to swim in the mainstream and some guidance for their efforts to do so.

Simultaneous attention to all three levels of needs is necessary, but dealing with the first two levels, which are more difficult than the third, requires much more effort. When the third level monopolizes attention, problems usually result because it is easy to forget that anything done at this level should contribute to meeting higher priority needs. When institutions focus their responses primarily on third-level needs, they are, in effect, telling black students that all they can look forward to is acceptance as tokens. In other words, the message often is that blacks may have some or all of the things that require no real effort or change by the college but may expect few, if any, of the basic changes which black students see as crucial.

There is evidence that third-level needs are getting most attention. What most black students want most has an almost inverse relationship to what they get. Table 6.4 indicates the contrast between changes they feel would "improve the experience of black students" and changes that they feel "have been made or could be made as a result of group activity." It is understandable that black students take what they can get. It also is understandable that they resent their inability to get what they need.

Providing what black students need most is difficult. It also is the way to make up for a late start toward equal opportunity at predominantly white colleges. Providing what is least necessary, but expedient, is easy, but it also is the way to make a late start a false start as well.

2. Financial aid should be maintained at current levels or increased.
3. The predictability of financial aid should be increased.
4. The emphasis on loans in the aid package should be decreased for those whose family income is less than $5,000.

Some of the most important conclusions of this study involve money. Sixty-eight percent of black students rely on grants or loans as their primary source of funds. Seventy-three percent of black students work at one or more jobs in order to make ends meet. Since there are limits to aid budgets and to anyone's ability to work while attending college, but apparently no limit to increasing costs, almost half of the black students worry about not having enough money to complete their education. The scope and intensity of that worry will increase as sources of aid are reduced, emphasis is shifted from grants to loans, or uncertainty about the supply of money is increased. If those developments occur, many blacks will fail to complete, or even start, college careers. Worry about money can hinder academic performance and force students from college before their last penny is spent. A substantial, sustained investment in trained black manpower is long overdue in this country. Reductions in the supply of money will produce reductions in the supply of black professionals at a time when significant progress is being made for the first time.

TABLE 6.4

	Desired Change	Rank	Actual or Possible Change	Rank
More recruitment of black students/staff	59	1st	9	5th & 7th
More financial aid, especially for blacks	41	2nd	—	—
Curriculum changes, especially expansion of Black Studies	38	3rd	32	1st
More remedial programs and tutoring	24	4th	8	8th
Purge racists and eliminate discrimination	15	5th	4	9th
More black activities, social life, culture	14	6th	18	2nd
Black lounge, center, etc.	1	10th	10	4th
All-black housing	1	11th	—	—
Black student organization	—	—	16	3rd
More representation in student government	—	—	9	5th

5. The number of black students in predominantly white colleges should continue to increase dramatically.
6. The number of black staff members in predominantly white colleges should increase dramatically.
7. Colleges should guard against increased hostility toward blacks as their numbers increase.
8. Colleges should recruit black students of diverse backgrounds and interests rather than concentrate most of their attention on those with multiple disadvantages.

Expanding the number of black students, faculty members, and administrators is listed as an important change most often by both staff and students. This is true because, even in colleges where there is relatively high black enrollment or a relatively large black staff, the percentage of blacks in college communities seldom approximates the percentage in the national, regional, or state populations. The recommendation regarding hostility is necessary because data in this study reflect much more discrimination in colleges which have larger percentages of black enrollment; and the next one, because of the prevalence of stereotypes which portray blackness as universally synonomous with many other differences from the majority of students. The data here clearly demonstrates that blacks are not all the same, so it is not necessary to recruit a homogeneous, multiply disadvantaged group. The data also indicate that where recruitment policies and/or chance produce a homogeneous group that fits stereotypes the results are disastrous.

9. Colleges should include the study of blacks in their curriculums either through specific courses on the topic or through revision of existing courses.

It is appropriate that black students react strongly to the continued lack of opportunity to get a realistic picture of the achievements, problems, and prospects of blacks in America and elsewhere. Black Studies alone is not an answer because standard courses which ignore or caricature blacks will remain a strong irritant.

10. Colleges should provide academic support to black students who need it.

11. Colleges should be sure that any special help is designed to help black students meet existing standards rather than to foster tolerance for a kind of second-class academic citizenship.

Data from this study indicates that most black students feel they can succeed academically without special help. It indicates that background characteristics such as low family income and little or no higher education in the family are not accurate predictors of the need for academic help. The data also suggests that small amounts of help suffice in many cases. Finally, the data reflects the fact that some forms of special treatment are offensive. It appears that help given without condescension or implications of inferiority is well received. On the other hand, help that consists of lowered standards provokes negative or ambivalent reactions.

12. Colleges should encourage black students to pursue a variety of majors.

13. Colleges should provide realistic advice about a broad range of career options and educational experiences which lead to them.

14. Colleges should involve whites as well as blacks extensively in advising and counseling black students.

Many rewarding and useful careers, especially those in technical and scientific fields, are not being pursued by blacks. Evidence of their attractiveness and feasibility for blacks is being developed and must be conveyed to black students. Unfortunately, that type of information is not always available to the young and relatively inexperienced blacks who often are assigned to deal with any and all problems of black students. Data from this study indicates that black students can be influenced by whites as well as blacks. There is, therefore, no reason to channel all queries from black students to a few overburdened black staff members. When whites have expertise and are willing to share it, they can advise black students effectively.

    15. Colleges should maintain channels of communication with more than a few "spokesmen" among their black students.

Data from this study indicates clearly that a tremendous variety of opinion exists among black students. It is unlikely that a realistic picture of those opinions can be obtained from a few individuals.

    16. Colleges should plan ahead in dealing with blacks rather than drift from crisis to crisis.

An example of failure in this area is the tendency of colleges to increase black enrollment significantly without increasing black staff representation past the token stage. This predictably leads to demands for more black staff and more black input in decision making along with bitterness on the part of students. Equal opportunity should be important enough to merit long-range planning.

In addition to recommendations for colleges, this study suggests two general recommendations for black students. These recommendations supplement the obvious corollaries to recommendations for colleges such as the importance of using all expertise available in making decisions about majors and careers.

    17. Young blacks should shop around carefully before enrolling in a college.

The amount of actual and anticipated transferring revealed by this study suggests that more careful "shopping" is in order. For the overwhelming majority who are not recruited by any college but who choose their college on the basis of proximity to home or net cost, collecting information about a variety of colleges is the main problem. For all prospective students critical evaluation of the information they obtain is an additional problem, but this type of evaluation is particularly important to those who are recruited. No matter how attractive a recruiter's pitch is, detailed examination of conditions for blacks at his school and other schools is worth the trouble. A little skepticism may prevent a student from being type-cast as one of the noble savages in some missionary's melodrama.

    18. Black students should struggle primarily for changes which will be most meaningful to their educational experience even if colleges resist those changes strongly while making other changes easy to obtain.

Whether the motives of colleges are malicious or not, they naturally will be more reluctant to make fundamental changes than to make cosmetic changes. Moreover, evidence from this study and news reports suggests that a series of peripheral victories may lead not to bigger victories but to a backlash which blocks attainment of more important objectives.

A final set of observations should be made. None of the recommendations here is intended to apply to all colleges or to provide "how to do it" instructions. Effective implementation of changes on any given campus must be based on information about that college and its students as well as information about groups of similar colleges and students. The Educational Policy Center is aware of this. It, therefore, is working with individual colleges to generate the necessary specific information and to help initiate constructive change. Those efforts can be much more productive now that the general data presented here is available.

NOTES

1. Because of the controversy about the practices of more selective colleges [see publications by Martin Kilson ("The Black Experience at Harvard," The New York Times Magazine, September 2, 1973) and Thomas Sowell (Black Education, Myths and Tragedies, op. cit.)], it should be noted that the problem institutions identified in this study were in the "less selective" category.

2. An example of an unnecessary obstacle placed in the path of black students is the common practice of advising them to avoid language courses because they will do poorly in them. Recent research at Ohio State indicates that the opposite is true. Blacks in the sample earned their best grades in language courses. (Human Behavior, December 1973, p. 47.)

3. Thomas Sowell, op. cit., p. 299.

METHODOLOGY

EPC's 1972-73 study of black undergraduates in white colleges is based on 979 completed interviews at forty colleges and universities.

Selection of the Institutions

The sampling universe covered all four-year colleges and universities in the continental United States with 51 percent or more white enrollment. The institutions were stratified by sponsorship (public or private). Within each of those strata, a second stratification was based on size (smallest total enrollment to largest).* Within each of the resulting strata, a third stratification was based on the percentage of black enrollment (lowest to highest).† Within each of the final strata, the institutions were arrayed by geographic location. Selection of the colleges and universities where interviews were to be conducted was completed by picking randomly within each stratification.

Selection of the Respondents

At each institution quotas were established for a minimum number of respondents from each college year (freshman, sophomore, etc.). In addition, interviewers were instructed to pick randomly within class-year strata or to seek diversity in sex, college major, and extracurricular interests if a list of black students could not be obtained.

Other Technical Information

Daniel Yankelovich, Inc., the nationally known survey research firm which conducted pre-election polling for The New York Times and Time magazine in 1972, assisted in the design of the study and

---

*Small: 0-4,999; Medium: 5,000-9,999; Large: 10,000+.
†Low: Up to 2.0%; Medium: 2.1%-4.0%; High: 4.1% and over.

handled the data processing. Invaluable assistance in conducting the study also was provided by a National Advisory Committee and EPC's Board of Directors. Lists of the membership of those groups appear in the front matter.

A list of sampling points and a reproduction of the questionnaire used in interviewing also follow.

Sampling Points

Ball State University
California State University (Hayward)
Campbell College
Central Connecticut State College
Clarion State College
Cleveland State University
Delaware Valley College of Science and Agriculture
Drexel University
Eastern Michigan University
Furman University
Gardner-Webb College
Heidelberg College
Long Island University
Newark State College
North Adams State College
Ohio State University
Oregon State University
Parsons College
Rider College
Rutgers University
Sam Houston State University
St. Cloud State University
Southwest Missouri State College
Tulane University
University of California (Berkeley)
University of Cincinnati
University of Denver
University of Detroit
University of Georgia
University of Michigan
University of Minnesota
University of San Francisco
University of South Carolina
University of Southern Mississippi
University of Texas (Austin)

University of Virginia
University of Wisconsin
Valparaiso University
Washington University
William Paterson College

Educational Policy Center, Inc.
400 Madison Avenue
New York, New York 10017

Study #3949
December, 1972

STUDENT SURVEY INSTRUMENT

INTERVIEWER:

    This interview is part of a nationwide survey being conducted among black students at predominantly white colleges by the Educational Policy Center of New York City. The Center is a non-profit organization established by a group of black educators and professionals to help colleges provide the best possible experience for black students. In this current survey, the Educational Policy Center hopes to develop a picture of the life of black students at predominantly white colleges and to use that information to develop policy and program suggestions.

    This interview should take approximately 45 minutes. Many of the questions are intentionally open-ended, and I urge you to respond as completely and in as much detail as you desire. Incidentally, your name will not be used in any way in reporting the results of this survey.

1-
2-
3-

Name of Student: _____ C.F. #: _____

4- 5- 6- 7- 8- 9- 10-

College: _____

College Year: First 11-1   Second -2   Third -3   Fourth -4

College Address: _____ City: _____ State: _____

College Telephone No.: _____

Permanent Address: _____ City: _____ State: _____

77

Name of Interviewer: _____

Date of Interview: _____ Time of Interview: _____ to ____

For Office Use Only:

Verified by: _ _____

Date: _____

Comments: _____

EDUCATIONAL POLICY CENTER STUDY

1. Could you think back for a moment and try to remember what you
   expected college to be like before you got here. In what ways has
   it turned out to be different from what you expected? (DO NOT
   READ ITEMS BELOW, BUT CIRCLE AS MANY AS ARE MEN-
   TIONED)

	How Different From Expectation	
	More or Better	Less or Poorer
ASPECT OF COLLEGE LIFE	Than Expected	Than Expected
1. Intellectual demands/academic challenge of college	12-1	13-1
2. Number of blacks in student body	-2	-2
3. Race relations	-3	-3
4. Individual freedom and privacy	-4	-4
5. Living conditions: dorms, food, etc.	-5	-5
6. Social life, extracurricular activities	-6	-6
7. Attention to individuals, help with problems	-7	-7
8. Student body's awareness, involvement, radicalism	-8	-8
9. Ability to live within planned budget	-9	-9
0. Similarity to high school	-0	-0
x. Other: _____	-x	-x

14-

2a. How did you decide to go to college? (HAND CARD A) Which things listed on the card influenced your decision? Just read the letters of those which apply.

b. Which one of these factors would you say was most important?

FACTORS	Affected Decision to Attend	One Most Important Factor
a. Career plans required college degree	15-1	16-1
b. Always wanted to go/decided as child/natural thing	-2	-2
c. Family expected it/wanted it/ made it possible	-3	-3
d. High school teachers or counselors expected/wanted/ made it possible	-4	-4
e. Friends all were going and made me want to: peer influence	-5	-5
f. Community leaders or family friends expected/wanted/ made it possible	-6	-6
g. Increased economic opportunity	-7	-7
h. This college sought me out/ provided special program	-8	-8
i. This college gave scholarship/ made financial arrangements	-9	-9
j. Other(s): _____	-0	-0

3a. How would you rate your academic preparation for college-level work? Was it:

1. Excellent	(SKIP TO Q. 4)	18-1
2. Good		-2
3. Fair	(GO ON TO Q. 3b)	-3
4. Poor		-4

b. (IF ANSWER WAS "FAIR" OR "POOR", ASK) In what subject areas or skills was your preparation inadequate? (DO NOT READ LIST)

1. Science	19-1
2. English	-2
3. Math	-3
4. Reading	-4

5. Writing   -5
6. Study habits; knowing how to use my time   -6
7. All areas; generally unprepared   -7
8. Other: _____   -8

4a. Some people we talk to say jobs, independent study, or other
    experiences outside their classroom education in high school
    helped them prepare for college. How about you?

1. Yes, outside experiences helped   (GO ON TO Q. 4b)   20-1
2. No, no helpful experiences outside (SKIP TO Q. 5)
   classroom   ⎤   -2
3. Other: _____   ⎦   -3

b. (HAND CARD B) Which of these things were helpful to you in
   preparing for college? Just read me the letters of those that
   apply to you.

a. Unassigned reading; independent studying I did on my own 21-1
b. Tutoring or study help by high school teachers outside
   class   -2
c. Tutoring or study help by someone besides teachers   -3
d. Work: jobs I held after school or in summer   -4
e. Special pre-enrollment preparation offered by this
   college   -5
f. Other: _____   -6

5a. If you had it to do over again, would you prepare for col-
    lege in the same way or a different way?

1. Different   (GO ON TO Q. 5b)   22-1
2. Same   ⎤   (SKIP TO Q. 6)   -2
3. Not Sure   ⎦   -3

5b. (HAND CARD C) What things on the card would you do
    differently?

a. More emphasis on basic skills: spelling, arithmetic,
   vocabulary, punctuation, etc.   23-1
b. More effort to learn how to think independently or
   theoretically   -2
c. Learn to read more rapidly, how to skim material
   and pick out essential points   -3
d. Learn to express my ideas better in writing or
   speaking   -4

e. Acquire more self-discipline: learn how to allocate
   time better or work on my own better   -5
f. Acquire more self-confidence: be more aware of
   my own special abilities   -6
g. Learn more about black history and accomplishments of other blacks   -7
h. Take studies in general more seriously: not just
   try to get by or do well in the short run   -8
i. Other things: _____   -9
                                                               24-

6. (HAND CARD D) Which three or four characteristics of this college were important in your decision
   to come here? Just read off the letters of those
   which apply in your case.

a. General reputation or academic standing   25-1
b. Curriculum or faculty in one field or department   -2
c. Scholarships or other financial assistance   -3
d. Proximity to home   -4
e. Large black population   -5
f. Low cost   -6
g. Size of student body   -7
h. Knew some people who were enrolled here   -8
i. Other (specify): _____   -9
                                                               26-

7a. Did you ever attend or consider going to a black
    college?

1. Yes, I considered it   27-1
2. Yes, I previously attended ⎤(GO ON TO Q. 7b)   -2
3. No   ⎦(SKIP TO Q. 8)   -3

7b. What made you decide not to (attend) (remain at) a black
    college? (DO NOT READ LIST)

1. Inadequate financial assistance   28-1
2. Too far away   -2
3. Didn't want to go to school in the South   -3
4. Black schools not as strong academically   -4
5. At a black school I would have played more and worked
   less: been distracted   -5
6. Employment opportunities are better for graduates of
   white schools   -6

81

7. My career interest is in a mostly white field, so I
   wanted to learn to function in predominantly
   white settings   -7
8. Didn't know much about black colleges   -8
9. Parents, advisors, or teachers didn't recommend
   black college   -9
0. Other: _____   -0
                                                                    29-

8. Do you think you were admitted to this college under
   special circumstances based on your race?

1. Yes/Probably/Perhaps   (GO ON TO Q. 9)   30-1
2. No   (SKIP TO Q. 10)   -2

9. (IF YES) Have the special circumstances had any
   major effect on your life here? (DO NOT READ LIST)

1. None so far   31-1
2. Feel like an outsider: isolated, alienated   -2
3. Pushed toward a certain major/career regardless
   of personal preferences   -3
4. Resentment by whites: idea that blacks get too much   -4
5. Not challenged; expected to be dumb, looking for
   easy way, etc.   -5
6. Other: _____   -6

10a. Do you think there is any likelihood that you will drop
    out of this college sometime before you graduate?

1. Yes/Perhaps   32-1
2. No   -2
3. Not Sure   -3

b. Why do you say that?   33-
                                                                    34-

10c. Of those black students who entered college here in
    your class, what percent (approximately) have left?

    (WRITE ACTUAL PERCENT) _____   35-

d. As far as you know, what are the three or four most
   common reasons that cause black students here to
   leave? (DO NOT READ LIST)

82

1. Academic reasons: pressure, poor preparation, etc.   36-1
2. Financial reasons   -2
3. Black-white friction, racism, etc.   -3
4. Frustration, confusion, isolation, etc.   -4
5. Bad habits, goofing off, etc.   -5
6. Want to transfer to other schools   -6
7. Other: _____   -7

11a. Do you have any concern about your ability to meet the costs of your college education?

   1. Yes/Some   (GO ON TO Q. 11b)   37-1
   2. No/None   (SKIP TO Q. 11c)   -2

  b. (IF YES) What makes you concerned? (DO <u>NOT</u> READ LIST)

   1. Cutbacks in special programs for blacks and other minorities   38-1
   2. Smaller amount of aid available each year   -2
   3. Extra money promised but not delivered   -3
   4. Amount of aid tied to grades; required average hard to maintain   -4
   5. Not enough for personal expenses. (Examples: _____)   -5
   6. Other: _____   -6

  c. (IF NO) Why aren't you worried? (DO <u>NOT</u> READ LIST)

   1. Adequate family resources   39-1
   2. Four-year scholarship   -2
   3. Good job(s)   -3
   4. Other: _____   -4

12a. (HAND CARD E) How would you describe yourself in terms of these things compared to other students in general? For example, is your class attendance better than, about as good as, or worse than most other students'?

	Better or More than	As Good or As Much as	Worse or Less than
a. Class attendance	40-1	41-1	42-1
b. Class participation	-2	-2	-2

		Better or More than	As Good or As Much as	Worse or Less than
c.	Extra, non-assigned	-3	-3	-3
	reading	-3	-3	-3
d.	Study habits	-4	-4	-4
e.	Need for special academic			
	help	-5	-5	-5

b. What kinds of activities do you participate in?
(DO NOT READ LIST)

1. Black organizations on campus   43-1
2. Student government   -2
3. Athletics   -3
4. Radio station, newspaper, etc.   -4
5. Club, choir, etc.   -5
6. Tutoring, advising   -6
7. Political activities off campus   -7
8. Service activities off campus   -8
9. Other:_____   -9
     44-

c. (HAND CARD F) What type of contact do you have
with faculty outside class?

a. Classwork-related only   45-1
b. About extra projects or reading   -2
c. General academic subjects   -3
d. Job-career prospects   -4
e. Social   -5
f. More with black faculty/little with white
    faculty   -6
g. Little or none   -7
h. Other:_____   -8

d. Have you received special academic help here?

1. Yes   (GO ON TO Q. 12e)   46-1
2. No   (SKIP TO Q. 12f)   -2

12e. (IF YES) How would you evaluate that help?
Was it: (READ LIST)

1. Insufficient   47-1
2. Adequate   -2
3. Too much: required remediation I didn't need   -3

f. (IF NO) How did you respond to the lack of help?
    (READ LIST)

1. Okay, I don't need it   48-1
2. Badly, I need it but it's not available   -2

13a. Do you feel that there is intense academic competition
     here among students? Please explain your answer.   49-
                                                              50-
                                                              51-

b. Has this had any effect on you personally?

1. Yes/Some   (GO ON TO Q. 13c)   52-1
2. No   ⎤   (SKIP TO Q. 14)   -2
3. Not Sure   ⎦   -3

c. (IF YES) What effect? (DO NOT READ LIST)

1. Increased motivation to study   53-1
2. Work harder to compete with whites   -2
3. Undermined self-confidence   -3
4. Other:_____   -4

d. (IF YES) Has this influenced the way you pick your
    courses or professors?

1. Yes   (GO ON TO Q. 13e)   54-1
2. No   -2
3. Not Sure   (SKIP TO Q. 14)   -3

e. (IF YES) How?   55-
                                                              56-

14. (HAND CARD G) When you have the types of
     problems listed on the card, to whom do you turn
     for help?

SOURCES	Aca-demic	Per-sonal	Finan-cial	Job/Career	Adminis-trative ("Red tape")
a. Other black student(s)	57-1	58-1	59-1	60-1	61-1
b. Black professor(s)	-2	-2	-2	-2	-2
c. White professor(s)	-3	-3	-3	-3	-3
d. Black counselor(s)	-4	-4	-4	-4	-4

SOURCES	Academic	Personal	Financial	Job/Career	Administrative ("Red tape")
e. white counselor(s)	-5	-5	-5	-5	-5
f. Black administrator(s)	-6	-6	-6	-6	-6
g. White administrator(s)	-7	-7	-7	-7	-7
h. Black student advisor, tutor, big brother, etc.	-8	-8	-8	-8	-8
i. Family	-9	-9	-9	-9	-9
j. Off-campus black friends	-0	-0	-0	-0	-0
k. No one	-x	-x	-x	-x	-x
l. Others: _____	-y	-y	-y	-y	-y
	62-	63-	64-	65-	66-

15a. Have you, in most cases, obtained the type of help you needed?

1. Yes	(SKIP TO Q. 16)		67-1
2. No ⎤	(GO ON TO Q. 15b)		-2
3. Not Sure⎦			-3

b. (IF NO or NOT SURE) Why?

68-

69-

16. Which faculty member(s) has (have) been most influential on your life here? (RECORD FULL NAME AND DEPT.) (PROBE: How? or Why?

Name	Dept.	Position	Race
		70-	71-
		72-	73-
		74-	75-
			80-1

17a. What is your living arrangement here? (DO NOT READ LIST, BUT PROBE FOR RACIAL MAKE-UP OF HOUSING)

1. Dormitory that mixes whites and blacks   4-1
2. All-black or minority dormitory, floor, or wing   -2
3. Private off-campus apartment or rooming house   -3
4. University married-student housing   -4
5. Other: _____   -5

b. What living arrangement would you prefer? (DO
   NOT READ LIST, BUT PROBE FOR PREFERRED
   RACIAL MAKE-UP)

1. Dormitory that mixes whites and blacks   5-1
2. All-black or minority dormitory, floor, or wing   -2
3. Private off-campus apartment or rooming house   -3
4. University married-student housing   -4
5. Other: _____   -5

c. Why would that be better for you?

                                                              6-
                                                              7-

18a. Have you ever held down a job during the school
     year while you've been at college?

1. Yes   (GO ON TO Q. 18b)   8-1
2. No   (SKIP TO Q. 19a)   -2

b. (IF YES) Are you currently holding down a job?

1. Yes   (GO ON TO Qs. 18c-f)   9-1
2. No   (SKIP TO Q. 19a)   -2

c. (IF YES TO Q. 18b) Is your work:

1. On campus job(s) only   10-1
2. Off campus job(s) only   -2
3. Several jobs both on and off campus   -3

18d. (IF YES TO Q. 18b) About how many hours a
     week have you worked at it?

     No. of hours: _____   11-

e. (IF YES TO Q. 18b) Has holding a job affected
   your college experience?

1. Yes   (GO ON TO Q. 18f)   12-1
2. No   ⎤   -2
3. Not Sure   ⎦   (SKIP TO Q. 19a)   -3

f. (IF YES TO Q. 18e) How has a job affected you?

1. Positively.   (Comments:)   13-1
2. Negatively.   (Comments:)   -2
                                                            14-
                                                            15-

19a. What is your social life like here? In other words,
     outside of classes and studying, what else do you do?
                                                            16-
                                                            17-

   b. How much does race influence your choice of
      friends and social activities? (READ LIST) Is it:

1. Dominant factor   18-1
2. Significant influence   -2
3. Little influence   -3

   c. Is this determined by your personal preferences,
      the overall situation, or what? (PROBE FOR FULL
      EXPLANATION)
                                                            19-
                                                            20-

   d. How much of your social life involves people who
      are not college students? (READ LIST)

1. Most   21-1
2. Some   -2
3. None   -3

19e. Why is that?   22-
                                                           23-

20a. Do you feel that you personally are able to
     influence the programs of this college that affect
     your life as a student here?

1. Yes   (GO ON TO Q. 20b)   24-1
2. No   ⎤   -2
3. Not Sure   ⎦   (SKIP TO Q. 20c)   -3

b. (IF YES) Why do you feel that why? Can you give any examples?

25-

26-

c. Can black students influence programs of this college through organized group efforts?

1. Yes	(GO ON TO Q. 20d)	27-1
2. Probably could, but haven't so far ⌉	(SKIP TO Q. 21)	-2
3. No		-3

d. Can you give examples of changes which have been made or could be made as a result of group activity?

28-

29-

21. How would you describe your overall reaction to this college thus far? (READ LIST)

1. Very satisfied	30-1
2. Somewhat satisfied	-2
3. Dissatisfied	-3

22. (HAND CARD H) Have the characteristics of this college listed on the card had <u>positive</u>, <u>negative</u>, or <u>insignificant</u> effect on your overall reaction to this college?

CHARACTERISTICS	Positive	Negative	Insignificant
a. Size of student body	31-1	32-1	33-1
b. Region of country	-2	-2	-2
c. Kind of place (urban, rural, etc.)	-3	-3	-3
d. Academic curriculum	-4	-4	-4
e. Size of classes	-5	-5	-5
f. Supportive services (counseling, tutoring, etc.)	-6	-6	-6
g. Percentage black enrollment	-7	-7	-7
h. Black faculty and administrative presence	-8	-8	-8
i. Accessibility of faculty members and administrators	-9	-9	-9

89

CHARACTERISTICS	Positive	Negative	Insignificant
j. Overt attempts to be responsive to the needs of blacks	-0 34-	-0 35-	-0 36-

23a. Have you been the victim of any racial discrimination in any aspects of your experience here?

1. Yes/Probably   (GO ON TO Q. 23b)   37-1
2. No   (SKIP TO Q. 24a)   -2

b. What do you have in mind? How did that happen?
38-
39-

24a. Do you think you have received any special favorable treatment because of your race in any aspects of your experience here?

1. Yes/Probably   (GO ON TO Q. 24b)   40-1
2. No   (SKIP TO Q. 25a)   -2

b. (IF YES) How did that make you feel? What effect did it have on you?
41-
42-

25a. Do you think this college really cares about having black students here?

1. Yes   43-1
2. No   -2
3. Not Sure   -3
44-
45-

b. How has this attitude or policy affected you?
(DO NOT READ LIST)

1. Not very much at all; expected it   46-1
2. Bitter/disillusioned/discouraged   -2
3. More determined to succeed   -3
4. More aware of need for black unity   -4
5. Other: _____   -5

26a. What are your plans after graduation from college?
(DO NOT READ LIST, BUT PROBE FOR DETAILS
AS INDICATED)

1. Graduate school—   47-1
   Subject area:
   Degree goal:
2. Work—   -2
   Type:
3. Work and Graduate School—   -3
   Type job:
   Type graduate program:
4. Other: _____   -4

b. Has your college experience changed your post-
graduate plans at all?

1. Yes   48-1
2. No   -2
3. Not Sure   -3

27. If you were the chief administrator of this college,
are there any new programs or policies you would
initiate to improve the experience of black students
here? (DO NOT READ LIST)

1. More recruitment of blacks (students, faculty, etc.)   49-1
2. More financial aid, especially for blacks   -2
3. More remedial programs and tutoring   -3
4. Expand black studies   -4
5. Purge racists from staff   -5
6. Other: _____   -6

DEMOGRAPHIC SECTION

INTERVIEWER:

Now I would like to use the last few minutes of this interview
to ask you some short-answer questions about yourself.

1. Age: _____   50-

2. (BY OBSERVATION)
   Male   51-1
   Female   -2

91

3a. Between the ages of 5 and 15, did you live predomi-
    nantly in a:

1. Large city   (more than 100,000 at that time)   52-1
2. Small city   (100,000 or less at that time)   -2
3. Suburban area   -3
4. Rural area   -4

b. What state was it in? _____   53-

4. Did either of your parents go to college, even if
   they didn't graduate?

1. Both   54-1
2. Father only   -2
3. Mother only   -3
4. Neither   -4

5. Did an older brother or sister of yours go to college
   before you?

1. Yes   55-1
2. No, they didn't attend   -2
3. No, I have no older brother or sister   -3

6a. What kind of secondary school did you graduate
    from?

1. Public high school   56-1
2. Private, non-sectarian school   -2
3. Parochial school (any denomination)   -3

6b. Where was it located?

    City/Town: _____   57-
    State: _____

7. Which of the following ranges best describes your
   parents' current annual income from all sources?
   (HAND CARD I) Just read me the letter of the
   range that applies.

a. Less than $5,000   58-1
b. $5,000-9,999   -2
c. 10,000-14,999   -3

92

d. 15,000-24,999   -4
e. 25,000 and up   -5

8. Are you:

1. Single   59-1
2. Married   -2
3. Single, but living with someone   -3
4. Divorced   -4
5. Separated   -5
6. Widowed   -6

9. What is your major field of study here?

 _____   60-

10. What is your academic average here?
(IF SCHOOL IS NOT ON A LETTER GRADE
SYSTEM, ASK) What is a perfect grade
average?

 _____ of a possible _____   61-

11a. How many colleges did you apply to?

 Actual number: _____   62-

11b. How many acceptances did you receive?

 Actual number: _____   63-

12a. Have you previously attended another college?

1. Yes   (GO ON TO Q. 12b) 64-1
2. No   (SKIP TO Q. 13a)   -2

b. (IF YES) Which one(s)? Where located?

 _____ in _____ 65-

 _____ in _____ 66-

c. (IF YES) Did that school (those schools) have a
higher proportion of black students than this one?

1. Yes, had higher proportion   67-1
2. No, had lower proportion   -2
3. Same proportion   -3

d. Did you transfer directly to this college or not?

1. Yes, transferred directly   (SKIP TO Q. 13a)   68-1
2. No, did not come directly   (GO ON TO Q. 12e)   -2

e. (IF NO) What did you do in the interim period?

1. Work   69-1
2. Travel   -2
3. Illness   -3
4. Other: _____   -4

13a. What are the sources of the money you use to go to
school? (HAND CARD J AND RECORD ANSWERS
BELOW)

b. (IF MORE THAN ONE SOURCE) I'm not going to ask
you for the amount, but could you rank the sources
from most to least in terms of the amount of money they
provide? Which provides the largest share? (PRO-
CEED TO RANK ALL SOURCES USED)

SOURCES	13a (Circle those Used)	13b (Rank those Used)
a. Family	70-1	71-
b. Scholarship from school	-2	72-
c. Scholarship from other source	-3	73-
d. Loan from school	-4	74-
e. Loan from bank, credit union	-5	75-
f. Loan from other source	-6	76-
g. Personal savings from summer jobs, pre-college jobs, gifts, etc.	-7	77-
h. Wages from jobs held during college	-8	78-
i. Other:	-9	79-

DATA AS COMPARED TO NATIONAL NORMS

Region and Sponsorship

	Nat'l. Norm	Region				Sponsorship	
		NE	MW	S	W	Public	Private
Age:							
17-18 years	23	17	21	35	17	17	34
19-20 years	41	43	46	37	32	43	37
21-22 years	21	20	23	17	21	22	17
23-26 years	12	17	7	9	21	14	8
27-35 years	3	2	3	2	6	3	2
Sex:							
Male	56	53	61	55	52	55	58
Female	44	47	39	45	48	45	42
Between the ages of 5 and 15, lived predominantly in a:							
Large city	56	45	75	33	73	54	62
Small city	23	28	14	33	18	27	15
Suburban area	10	17	8	11	1	9	12
Rural area	8	4	2	21	5	7	9
Home was located in:							
Same area as secondary school	89	85	89	94	91	90	87
Different area from secondary school	7	7	10	4	7	6	9
Secondary school was located in:							
Same area as college	78	86	69	83	76	86	63
Different area from college	20	11	29	15	20	12	35
Previously attended another college:							
Yes	25	21	24	18	47	26	22
No	69	59	74	81	53	65	75
If yes, it was a:							
Two-year public college	49	49	31	33	85	57	32
Two-year private college	6	10	6	10	—	5	9
Black college	10	15	10	19	2	13	5
Four-year, white, public college	26	31	36	26	9	23	34
Four-year, white, private college	13	14	16	9	10	10	18
Parents who attended college:							
Both	16	10	18	15	26	16	15
Father only	10	9	12	7	15	10	12
Mother only	15	15	15	14	16	16	13
Neither	59	66	56	65	42	58	60
Older brother(s) or sister(s) attended college:							
Yes	45	35	46	53	45	44	45
No	30	39	30	26	22	32	27
No; have no older brother or sister	25	27	24	21	33	24	27
Range of family's current annual income:							
Less than $5,000	18	13	17	26	22	17	21
$ 5,000- 9,999	36	38	35	38	29	36	35
$10,000-14,999	25	31	24	20	29	27	22
$15,000-24,999	13	9	18	10	10	11	15
$25,000 and over	6	6	6	4	7	7	4
Major field of study:							
Social Sciences	17	21	15	16	20	17	18
Political Science and History	11	12	12	9	10	12	9
Business	15	11	13	18	18	15	13
Education	15	26	14	12	3	15	16
Biological Sciences	6	3	6	5	10	5	7
Engineering and Math	4	2	3	7	3	3	5
Physical Sciences	2	2	2	1	1	2	1
Health Professions (non-M.D.)	3	1	3	5	4	2	4
English	4	2	5	4	4	3	5
Fine Arts	4	4	5	5	4	4	6
Black Studies	1	1	—	1	1	1	—

(continued)

	Nat'l. Norm	Region				Sponsorship	
		NE	MW	S	W	Public	Private
Academic average:							
A	1	1	—	—	2	1	—
B	25	22	25	23	36	25	25
C	59	55	55	70	59	60	58
D or F	7	7	10	6	—	4	13
Plans after graduation from college:							
Graduate school	45	45	43	46	48	44	47
Work	34	31	37	35	33	35	32
Work and Graduate school	10	12	8	10	10	9	12
Main source of money used to go to college:							
Family	20	22	21	22	11	20	19
Scholarship from college	29	24	33	30	23	24	39
Scholarship from other source	16	29	11	11	13	16	16
Loan from college	11	3	13	11	20	13	6
Loan from bank or credit union	6	3	7	5	10	7	5
Loan from other source	3	4	4	4	—	3	5
Personal savings	4	5	3	4	2	4	2
Wages from jobs held during college	6	5	6	4	11	8	2
Veterans' benefits	3	2	1	2	8	3	1
Rating of academic preparation:							
Excellent	10	10	11	11	8	8	14
Good	38	36	33	53	29	38	38
Fair	29	30	27	27	36	31	25
Poor	23	24	28	10	27	22	23
Characteristics important in selecting this college:							
General reputation or academic standing	48	38	50	60	43	46	53
Curriculum or faculty in one field or department	26	25	22	31	30	25	29
Scholarships or other financial assistance	53	56	52	56	45	47	65
Proximity to home	50	52	50	46	54	58	34
Large black population	6	5	6	3	11	7	4
Low cost	20	20	17	29	8	29	—
Size of student body	14	8	18	17	7	10	21
Knew others who were enrolled here	27	21	31	29	27	29	24
Admitted under special circumstances based on race:							
Yes/Probably/Perhaps	50	61	45	42	55	46	59
No	50	39	55	58	45	54	41
If yes, major effects on life here:							
None so far	59	58	53	65	65	58	61
Feel like an outsider: isolated, alienated	16	10	25	20	5	14	19
Pushed toward certain major or career	4	1	6	5	4	4	4
Resented by whites: idea that blacks get too much	9	7	7	9	16	10	6
Unchallenged; expected to be dumb, etc.	9	9	7	4	19	10	7
Estimated black attrition rate:							
0–10 percent	41	24	38	69	36	39	46
10–25 percent	15	23	14	11	11	16	13
25–50 percent	14	23	17	7	3	15	13
50 percent or over	9	10	13	3	11	10	8
Unknown	16	19	16	6	31	16	18
Most common reasons for black attrition:							
Academic reasons: pressure, poor preparation, etc.	63	69	62	61	56	66	57
Financial reasons	50	40	64	42	45	50	48
Black-white friction, racism, etc.	24	22	17	28	37	23	25
Frustration, confusion, isolation, etc.	38	32	38	40	48	38	38
Concerned about ability to meet college costs:							
Yes	47	48	51	41	46	46	49
No	53	52	49	59	54	54	51
If yes, concerned about:							
Cutbacks in special programs for blacks/minorities	31	41	26	26	30	33	26
Smaller amount of aid available each year	40	35	43	34	54	43	36
Amount of aid tied to maintaining high grade average	12	5	14	23	4	6	23
Insufficient money for personal expenses	17	12	24	12	20	13	26
If no, unconcerned because of:							
Adequate family resources	33	30	34	41	23	34	33
Four-year scholarship	40	42	44	37	30	37	45
Good job(s)	11	9	7	13	19	13	6
Adequate financial aid	25	22	18	30	36	24	27
Activities participated in:							
Black organizations on campus	47	52	42	57	34	45	53
Student government, college committees, etc.	11	11	14	10	6	9	15

	Nat'l. Norm	Region				Sponsorship	
		NE	MW	S	W	Public	Private
Athletics	30	30	38	27	14	27	37
Radio station, newspaper, etc.	4	6	4	3	1	2	7
Club, choir, etc.	21	24	18	27	14	20	25
Tutoring, advising	7	9	8	4	7	7	8
Political activities off campus	5	4	6	5	7	4	7
Service activities off campus	10	16	8	8	5	10	9
None	25	27	20	20	44	30	17
Type of contact with faculty members outside class:							
Classwork-related only	36	27	39	43	32	36	36
Extra projects or reading	17	19	18	14	16	15	20
General academic subjects	20	28	16	19	18	21	18
Job/career prospects	14	16	15	12	7	13	15
Social	16	17	18	15	7	15	17
More with black faculty/Little with white faculty	22	31	20	16	19	25	16
Little or none	40	37	41	37	50	41	39
Special academic help received:							
Yes	34	36	36	22	47	33	36
No	66	64	64	79	53	67	64
If yes, evaluation of help received:							
Insufficient	23	29	21	13	25	25	20
Adequate	76	70	79	88	73	75	80
Too much: required remediation not needed	1	1	—	—	2	—	—
If no, response to lack of help:							
Ambivalent: help wasn't needed	79	80	79	79	72	78	79
Negative: help was needed but unavailable	17	15	16	16	25	17	15
Intense academic competition among students:							
Yes	59	58	56	55	77	61	56
No	36	38	38	39	22	35	38
Not sure	3	3	5	1	—	4	1
Effect on student personally:							
Some	62	58	62	63	69	63	61
None	35	42	34	33	30	35	36
Not sure	3	—	4	4	2	2	3
If some, resulted in:							
Increased motivation to study	46	36	50	61	37	44	51
Harder work to compete with whites	37	40	34	44	29	36	38
Undermined self-confidence	12	11	9	5	26	13	9
Decreased motivation to study	6	4	8	5	9	7	5
Current living arrangement:							
Interracial dormitory	48	33	63	62	11	41	61
All-black or minority dormitory, floor, wing	4	12	1	2	1	5	2
Private off-campus apartment or rooming house	24	14	22	25	47	28	15
Parents' home	18	35	9	6	32	21	12
Preferred living arrangement:							
Interracial dormitory	20	16	18	36	2	14	30
All-black or minority dormitory, floor, wing	15	16	18	14	9	15	15
Private off-campus apartment or rooming house	46	38	52	40	60	48	43
Parents' home	9	15	6	1	18	11	5
Influence of race on choice of friends and activities:							
Dominant influence	41	36	40	40	58	43	39
Significant influence	27	35	28	20	21	30	23
Little influence	31	28	32	40	20	27	39
Ability of organized black students to influence programs:							
Yes, they're able to	57	60	55	57	56	59	54
Probably could, but haven't so far	24	26	28	16	19	25	20
No, they're unable to	19	13	16	27	25	16	25
Overall reaction to this college:							
Very satisfied	8	8	7	9	8	8	7
Somewhat satisfied	56	50	59	64	45	55	57
Dissatisfied	36	42	34	26	45	35	36
Negative characteristics of this college:							
Low percentage black enrollment	60	71	53	61	57	59	63
Low black faculty and administrative presence	60	73	50	67	48	56	69

(continued)

(continued)

	Nat'l. Norm	NE	MW	S	W	Public	Private
			Region			Sponsorship	
Low accessibility of faculty and administrators	42	49	35	37	55	44	36
Lack of overt attempts to respond to blacks' needs	61	71	55	54	72	64	55
Victim of any aspect of racial discrimination here:							
Yes/Probably	49	46	50	43	59	50	46
No	51	54	50	56	41	50	54
Recipient of special favorable treatment because of race:							
Yes/Probably	27	29	28	24	23	26	29
No	73	70	72	75	77	74	71
If yes, reaction to special treatment:							
Positive	34	36	33	40	21	38	28
Negative	28	42	26	11	28	27	30
Ambivalent	14	5	11	17	39	13	15
Little or no reaction	12	6	15	20	—	10	15
College cares about having black students:							
Yes	18	16	22	23	5	16	23
No	67	73	62	58	80	68	63
Not sure	14	11	15	18	13	15	13
Changes which should be made for black students:							
More recruitment of black students and faculty	59	54	52	78	57	55	67
Revised admissions standards	4	4	1	2	12	5	1
More financial aid (especially for blacks)	41	33	43	43	48	43	38
Greater role for blacks in decision making	4	4	4	2	11	4	4
More remedial programs and tutoring	24	35	24	10	30	27	19
Curriculum changes to reflect relevance	5	4	5	3	10	5	7
Expansion of Black Studies	33	29	28	46	29	29	40
Purge of racists from staff	15	10	14	22	12	14	16
All-black housing	1	2	1	—	2	1	2
Black lounge or Center	1	2	—	—	5	1	2
More black activities, social life, cultural events	14	20	10	15	14	14	14

COLLEGE DEMOGRAPHIC DATA

	Nat'l. Norm	NE	MW	S	W	Public	Private
Region:							
Northeast	27	100	—	—	—	29	24
Midwest	36	—	100	—	—	33	40
South	24	—	—	100	—	21	30
West	13	—	—	—	100	17	6
Sponsorship:							
Public	67	70	63	58	86	100	—
Private	33	30	37	42	14	—	100
Size:							
Small	35	43	37	42	—	11	82
Medium	23	26	14	29	29	30	8
Large	42	31	49	29	71	58	10
Percentage black enrollment:							
Low	16	7	5	38	24	16	16
Medium	30	19	28	62	—	23	44
High	54	74	67	—	76	61	39
Location:							
Central City	41	26	52	35	55	37	50
Other Urban	45	68	34	34	45	58	17
Non-metropolitan	14	6	14	31	—	4	33

	Nat'l. Norm	Location			Percentage Black Enrollment		
		MU	OU	NM*	Low	Med.	High
Age:							
17-18 years	23	17	24	34	30	32	16
19-20 years	41	45	40	33	36	42	43
21-22 years	21	20	21	22	19	16	23
23-26 years	12	13	12	9	10	9	15
27-35 years	3	4	3	2	4	2	3
Sex:							
Male	56	59	52	61	57	57	55
Female	44	41	48	39	33	43	45
Between the ages of 5 and 15, lived predominantly in a:							
Large city	56	68	49	46	49	51	62
Small city	23	18	27	23	23	26	21
Suburban area	10	7	12	12	11	10	10
Rural area	8	4	8	16	14	11	4
Home was located in:							
Same area as secondary school	89	89	88	93	90	89	89
Different area from secondary school	7	8	7	4	6	7	7
Secondary school was located in:							
Same area as college	78	80	85	50	76	80	78
Different area from college	20	18	13	46	22	20	19
Previously attended another college:							
Yes	25	28	20	28	21	18	29
No	69	70	67	70	78	79	61
If yes, it was a:							
Two-year public college	49	47	59	31	40	31	57
Two-year private college	6	5	5	11	5	11	5
Black college	10	13	9	7	12	13	9
Four-year, white, public college	26	26	27	24	38	24	24
Four-year, white, private college	13	12	15	11	10	15	13
Parents who attended college:							
Both	16	19	15	9	14	15	17
Father only	10	12	9	9	7	8	13
Mother only	15	16	13	17	13	14	16
Neither	59	53	63	64	65	64	54
Older brother(s) or sister(s) attended college:							
Yes	45	44	43	50	44	47	43
No	30	32	31	25	29	29	31
No; have no older brother or sister	25	24	26	26	26	24	26
Range of family's current annual income:							
Less than $5,000	18	21	16	21	22	25	14
$5,000-9,999	36	39	34	30	43	32	35
$10,000-14,999	25	19	30	28	17	23	29
$15,000-24,999	13	14	11	12	9	13	13
$25,000 and over	6	5	7	5	4	5	7
Major field of study:							
Social Sciences	17	16	19	15	16	16	19
Political Science and History	11	9	13	9	8	10	12
Business	15	18	11	15	18	16	13
Education	15	10	18	22	12	13	18
Biological Sciences	6	10	3	2	4	6	5
Engineering and Math	4	7	2	—	7	5	2
Physical Sciences	2	1	3	—	1	1	2
Health Professions (non-M.D.)	3	3	2	7	3	4	2
English	4	4	3	5	1	5	4
Fine Arts	4	4	5	6	5	6	3
Black Studies	1	1	1	—	—	1	1
Academic average:							
A	1	1	1	—	1	—	1
B	25	30	24	17	28	26	24

(continued)

(continued)

	Nat'l. Norm	Location			Percentage Black Enrollment		
		MU	OU	NM	Low	Med.	High
C	59	57	61	62	66	62	56
D or F	7	5	5	19	4	10	6
Plans after graduation from college:							
Graduate school	45	43	50	34	46	43	46
Work	34	34	30	47	26	40	33
Work and Graduate school	10	10	9	13	13	10	10
Main source of money used to go to college:							
Family	20	17	21	27	13	23	20
Scholarship from college	29	36	22	27	30	32	27
Scholarship from other source	16	16	19	8	11	15	18
Loan from college	11	9	14	6	22	11	8
Loan from bank or credit union	6	5	6	10	4	6	7
Loan from other source	3	3	3	6	4	2	4
Personal savings	4	3	4	3	2	4	4
Wages from jobs held during college	6	8	5	3	3	3	8
Veterans' benefits	3	2	3	2	3	1	3
Rating of academic preparation:							
Excellent	10	11	10	9	13	11	9
Good	38	33	39	50	43	45	33
Fair	29	27	31	27	26	25	32
Poor	23	28	20	14	18	19	26
Characteristics important in selecting this college:							
General reputation or academic standing	48	57	43	39	60	54	42
Curriculum or faculty in one field or department	26	27	24	31	29	32	22
Scholarships or other financial assistance	53	57	50	52	57	57	50
Proximity to home	50	55	49	40	36	46	56
Large black population	6	8	4	5	1	4	8
Low cost	20	22	20	11	13	26	18
Size of student body	14	9	16	18	23	13	11
Knew others who were enrolled here	27	23	28	38	25	30	27
Admitted under special circumstances based on race:							
Yes/Probably/Perhaps	50	49	54	40	53	48	51
No	50	51	46	60	47	53	49
If yes, major effects on life here:							
None so far	59	59	60	55	61	54	61
Feel like an outsider: isolated, alienated	16	15	14	27	10	19	16
Pushed toward certain major or career	4	5	2	5	5	6	3
Resented by whites: idea that blacks get too much	9	10	7	9	12	13	6
Unchallenged; expected to be dumb, etc.	9	10	8	6	14	6	8
Estimated black attrition rate:							
0-10 percent	41	37	41	54	61	48	31
10-25 percent	15	15	15	17	10	14	17
25-50 percent	14	10	20	10	7	12	18
50 percent or over	9	13	8	4	10	9	10
Unknown	16	22	13	8	6	14	21
Most common reasons for black attrition:							
Academic reasons: pressure, poor preparation, etc.	63	68	65	42	50	65	65
Financial reasons	50	53	47	47	42	47	53
Black-white friction, racism, etc.	24	16	29	32	29	25	22
Frustration, confusion, isolation, etc.	38	29	45	41	57	34	35
Concerned about ability to meet college costs:							
Yes	47	45	49	46	46	46	48
No	53	55	51	54	54	54	52
If yes, concerned about:							
Cutbacks in special programs for blacks/minorities	31	26	37	23	28	25	35
Smaller amount of aid available each year	40	42	41	33	40	42	39
Amount of aid tied to maintaining high grade average	12	14	7	24	19	16	8
Insufficient money for personal expenses	17	26	11	13	12	19	18
If no, unconcerned because of:							
Adequate family resources	33	33	33	36	30	39	31
Four-year scholarship	40	43	38	36	49	39	38
Good job(s)	11	13	9	11	12	8	12
Adequate financial aid	25	24	25	29	23	27	25

	Nat'l. Norm	Location			Percentage Black Enrollment		
		MU	OU	NM	Low	Med.	High
Activities participated in:							
Black organizations on campus	47	42	50	56	59	56	40
Student government, college committees, etc.	11	10	10	19	8	14	11
Athletics	30	28	27	44	27	35	28
Radio station, newspaper, etc.	4	3	3	9	3	7	3
Club, choir, etc.	21	19	21	30	20	28	18
Tutoring, advising	7	6	8	10	6	7	8
Political activities off campus	5	6	3	9	5	5	5
Service activities off campus	10	8	11	10	8	9	11
None	25	25	29	14	17	16	33
Type of contact with faculty members outside class:							
Classwork-related only	36	38	33	38	50	38	30
Extra projects or reading	17	16	17	22	11	18	18
General academic subjects	20	20	22	14	14	19	22
Job/career prospects	14	14	12	17	9	18	13
Social	16	13	17	21	11	17	17
More with black faculty/Little with white faculty	22	21	26	11	20	17	25
Little or none	40	44	39	34	32	44	41
Special academic help received:							
Yes	34	42	29	27	33	35	34
No	66	58	71	73	66	65	66
If yes, evaluation of help received:							
Insufficient	23	19	30	17	13	21	27
Adequate	76	81	69	81	84	79	73
Too much: required remediation not needed	1	—	1	1	4	—	—
If no, response to lack of help:							
Ambivalent: help wasn't needed	79	79	81	70	83	79	77
Negative: help was needed but unavailable	17	17	14	24	11	19	17
Intense academic competition among students:							
Yes	59	64	62	39	61	60	58
No	36	31	36	51	33	35	37
Not sure	3	5	2	1	1	2	4
Effect on student personally:							
Some	62	68	56	66	58	66	61
None	35	30	41	29	38	31	37
Not sure	3	2	3	5	4	3	2
If some, resulted in:							
Increased motivation to study	46	46	45	52	54	50	42
Harder work to compete with whites	37	36	32	64	40	37	36
Undermined self-confidence	12	15	10	8	13	8	14
Decreased motivation to study	6	8	6	—	6	7	6
Current living arrangement:							
Interracial dormitory	48	46	42	70	51	61	39
All-black or minority dormitory, floor, wing	4	1	7	4	4	2	5
Private off-campus apartment or rooming house	24	32	20	12	33	22	22
Parents' home	18	14	26	5	4	8	28
Preferred living arrangement:							
Interracial dormitory	20	16	17	39	27	28	13
All-black or minority dormitory, floor, wing	15	15	15	15	17	16	14
Private off-campus apartment or rooming house	46	53	43	37	45	45	48
Parents' home	9	8	12	1	1	3	15
Influence of race on choice of friends and activities:							
Dominant influence	41	48	38	35	37	47	40
Significant influence	27	27	29	22	23	24	30
Little influence	31	26	33	42	39	30	30
Ability of organized black students to influence programs:							
Yes, they're able to	57	61	55	53	46	67	55
Probably could, but haven't so far	24	24	25	18	20	17	28
No, they're unable to	19	15	20	28	34	16	16
Overall reaction to this college:							
Very satisfied	8	8	7	8	8	8	8
Somewhat satisfied	56	62	53	50	59	59	54
Dissatisfied	36	29	40	42	32	34	38

101

	Nat'l. Norm	Location			Percentage Black Enrollment		
		MU	OU	NM*	Low	Med	High
Negative characteristics of this college:							
Low percentage black enrollment	60	54	65	65	73	59	57
Low black faculty and administration	60	51	64	76	69	63	56
Low accessibility of faculty and administrators	42	38	45	41	39	36	46
Lack of overt attempts to respond to blacks' needs	61	60	62	60	53	58	65
Victim of any aspect of racial discrimination here:							
Yes/Probably	49	49	38	49	35	53	50
No	51	51	52	51	64	47	50
Recipient of special favorable treatment because of race:							
Yes/Probably	27	27	27	27	23	31	26
No	73	72	73	73	77	68	74
If yes, reaction to special treatment:							
Positive	34	40	32	23	42	36	31
Negative	28	22	32	33	20	25	32
Ambivalent	14	22	8	7	8	16	14
Little or no reaction	12	11	6	30	18	15	8
College cares about having black students:							
Yes	18	15	18	32	22	19	17
No	67	67	69	57	57	70	68
Not sure	14	17	13	12	21	12	14
Changes which should be made for black students:							
More recruitment of black students and faculty	59	53	60	77	83	64	49
Revised admissions standards	4	4	4	–	3	1	5
More financial aid (especially for blacks)	41	47	38	34	51	34	42
Greater role for blacks in decision making	4	7	3	2	2	4	5
More remedial programs and tutoring	24	23	28	13	18	18	30
Curriculum changes to reflect relevance	5	7	4	2	2	4	7
Expansion of Black Studies	33	25	33	55	54	38	23
Purge of racists from staff	15	13	11	33	21	19	10
All-black housing	1	2	–	1	1	3	–
Black lounge or Center	1	2	1	–	1	2	1
More black activities, social life, cultural events	14	10	18	17	16	13	15

COLLEGE DEMOGRAPHIC DATA

	Nat'l. Norm	Location			Percentage Black Enrollment		
		MU	OU	NM*	Low	Med	High
Region:							
Northeast	27	17	41	11	12	17	37
Midwest	36	45	27	36	10	33	44
South	24	21	18	53	58	50	–
West	13	18	13	–	20	–	19
Sponsorship:							
Public	67	60	87	21	66	51	76
Private	33	40	13	79	34	49	24
Size:							
Small	35	26	28	84	35	42	31
Medium	23	17	30	16	24	22	22
Large	42	57	42	–	41	36	46
Percentage black enrollment:							
Low	16	8	20	25	100	–	–
Medium	30	42	12	52	–	100	–
High	54	50	67	23	–	–	100
Location:							
Central City	41	100	–	–	21	57	39
Other Urban	45	–	100	–	58	18	55
Non-metropolitan	14	–	–	100	22	24	6

*MU = Major Urban; OU = Other Urban; NM = Non-Metropolitan.

102

	Nat'l. Norm	Sex		Family Income			
		Male	Female	0-4,999	5,000-9,999	10,000-14,999	15,000+
Age:							
17-18 years	23	17	29	22	18	24	31
19-20 years	41	38	45	37	43	42	41
21-22 years	21	26	14	20	24	19	17
23-26 years	12	14	10	14	11	14	9
27-35 years	3	4	2	5	4	1	2
Sex:							
Male	56	100	—	58	61	55	45
Female	44	—	100	42	39	45	55
Between the ages of 5 and 15, lived predominantly in a:							
Large city	56	58	54	52	57	52	66
Small city	23	22	25	19	26	24	21
Suburban area	10	8	13	8	8	15	7
Rural area	8	9	6	18	7	7	1
Home was located in:							
Same area as secondary school	89	88	91	92	90	88	89
Different area from secondary school	7	8	5	6	7	9	4
Secondary school was located in:							
Same area as college	78	74	84	67	84	81	74
Different area from college	20	24	14	30	14	17	23
Previously attended another college:							
Yes	25	28	20	30	22	24	23
No	69	65	73	68	73	64	70
If yes, it was a:							
Two-year public college	49	55	38	52	55	55	35
Two-year private college	6	5	8	4	8	2	6
Black college	10	8	14	16	8	2	22
Four-year, white, public college	26	21	36	20	30	21	37
Four-year, white, private college	13	12	14	14	13	13	8
Parents who attended college:							
Both	16	11	22	5	7	15	46
Father only	10	11	10	10	8	12	15
Mother only	15	12	18	9	12	21	16
Neither	59	66	50	76	73	52	23
Older brother(s) or sister(s) attended college:							
Yes	45	42	47	41	42	43	51
No	30	35	24	43	35	26	15
No; have no older brother or sister	25	22	29	15	23	30	34
Range of family's current annual income:							
Less than $5,000	18	19	18	100	—	—	—
$ 5,000-9,999	36	39	31	—	100	—	—
$10,000-14,999	25	25	26	—	—	100	—
$15,000-24,999	13	11	15	—	—	—	68
$25,000 and over	6	4	8	—	—	—	32
Major field of study:							
Social Sciences	17	15	21	20	17	18	16
Political Science and History	11	14	6	7	12	14	7
Business	15	18	10	19	13	12	17
Education	15	12	19	14	17	12	18
Biological Sciences	6	6	5	4	4	8	8
Engineering and Math	4	5	2	2	4	1	7
Physical Sciences	2	2	1	1	2	3	1
Health Professions (non-M.D.)	3	1	6	8	2	3	—
English	4	2	6	2	4	7	1
Fine Arts	4	4	4	5	6	2	5
Black Studies	1	1	—	3	—	—	—
Academic average:							
A	1	1	—	—	2	—	—
B	25	21	31	23	26	22	28

(continued)

103

	Nat'l. Norm	Sex Male	Female	Family Income 0- 4,999	5,000- 9,999	10,000- 14,999	15,000+
C	59	65	52	64	61	62	53
D or F	7	7	6	7	7	5	9
Plans after graduation from college:							
Graduate school	45	45	45	44	39	45	57
Work	34	34	34	39	32	37	31
Work and Graduate school	10	8	13	13	13	8	4
Main source of money used to go to college:							
Family	20	12	30	4	9	21	55
Scholarship from college	29	33	23	34	35	25	16
Scholarship from other source	16	14	19	28	19	12	6
Loan from college	11	11	11	19	8	13	5
Loan from bank or credit union	6	7	5	4	5	11	5
Loan from other source	3	3	4	1	6	4	1
Personal savings	4	5	1	3	4	5	2
Wages from jobs held during college	6	6	5	3	6	4	10
Veterans' benefits	3	4	—	4	3	2	1
Rating of academic preparation:							
Excellent	10	8	13	7	9	10	16
Good	38	36	41	34	38	41	39
Fair	29	29	29	23	29	34	27
Poor	23	27	17	35	24	14	20
Characteristics important in selecting this college:							
General reputation or academic standing	48	45	52	42	53	38	59
Curriculum or faculty in one field or department	26	26	26	31	25	21	31
Scholarships or other financial assistance	53	57	48	66	62	49	31
Proximity to home	50	46	54	41	52	51	55
Large black population	6	8	3	4	3	8	8
Low cost	20	20	20	17	21	22	17
Size of student body	14	12	15	11	14	11	19
Knew others who were enrolled here	27	29	25	29	27	22	34
Admitted under special circumstances based on race:							
Yes/Probably/Perhaps	50	53	46	57	55	50	35
No	50	47	54	43	45	50	65
If yes, major effects on life here:							
None so far	59	60	58	59	52	71	52
Feel like an outsider: isolated, alienated	16	17	15	22	12	12	28
Pushed toward certain major or career	4	5	2	3	6	1	7
Resented by whites: idea that blacks get too much	9	7	11	13	12	3	3
Unchallenged; expected to be dumb, etc.	9	9	8	8	12	4	8
Estimated black attrition rate:							
0-10 percent	41	38	46	40	45	36	41
10-25 percent	15	18	12	12	17	16	13
25-50 percent	14	16	12	14	11	18	17
50 percent or over	9	12	6	8	11	11	4
Unknown	16	12	22	20	11	18	20
Most common reasons for black attrition:							
Academic reasons: pressure, poor preparation, etc.	63	64	62	53	71	64	60
Financial reasons	50	48	52	49	47	48	57
Black-white friction, racism, etc.	24	23	25	23	22	26	25
Frustration, confusion, isolation, etc.	38	41	34	40	35	43	34
Concerned about ability to meet college costs:							
Yes	47	46	49	54	49	45	39
No	53	54	51	47	51	55	61
If yes, concerned about:							
Cutbacks in special programs for blacks/minorities	31	32	29	40	22	35	35
Smaller amount of aid available each year	40	36	45	44	38	40	39
Amount of aid tied to maintaining high grade average	12	12	12	12	19	7	3
Insufficient money for personal expenses	17	19	15	15	23	17	8
If no, unconcerned because of:							
Adequate family resources	33	24	46	10	20	35	68
Four-year scholarship	40	43	35	54	46	37	23

(continued)

	Nat'l. Norm	Sex		Family Income			
		Male	Female	0-4,999	5,000-9,999	10,000-14,999	15,000+
Good job(s)	11	12	9	6	10	12	13
Adequate financial aid	25	28	21	38	27	28	9
Activities participated in:							
Black organizations on campus	47	49	46	51	45	42	59
Student government, college committees, etc.	11	10	13	12	10	9	15
Athletics	30	44	13	31	31	27	34
Radio station, newspaper, etc.	4	5	2	3	4	4	5
Club, choir, etc.	21	18	25	22	21	18	29
Tutoring, advising	7	7	8	2	7	8	12
Political activities off campus	5	6	5	2	8	4	6
Service activities off campus	10	9	11	7	10	11	10
None	25	21	30	26	26	29	15
Type of contact with faculty members outside class:							
Classwork-related only	36	33	39	36	41	31	32
Extra projects or reading	17	13	22	15	17	18	19
General academic subjects	20	14	28	20	18	19	23
Job/career prospects	14	12	16	14	13	14	16
Social	16	17	14	17	13	15	21
More with black faculty/Little with white faculty	22	22	22	16	21	24	28
Little or none	40	44	35	47	38	44	32
Special academic help received:							
Yes	34	33	35	33	34	37	32
No	66	67	65	67	66	63	68
If yes, evaluation of help received:							
Insufficient	23	21	25	34	20	23	18
Adequate	76	78	74	64	79	77	83
Too much: required remediation not needed	1	1	—	2	—	—	—
If no, response to lack of help:							
Ambivalent: help wasn't needed	79	80	77	82	80	73	81
Negative: help was needed but unavailable	17	17	17	15	16	19	15
Intense academic competition among students:							
Yes	59	58	61	68	60	54	58
No	36	37	35	31	34	41	36
Not sure	3	3	3	1	4	2	4
Effect on student personally:							
Some	62	60	65	70	56	64	63
None	35	36	34	26	41	34	36
Not sure	3	3	2	4	3	2	1
If some, resulted in:							
Increased motivation to study	46	51	41	56	51	28	50
Harder work to compete with whites	37	38	35	38	37	40	33
Undermined self-confidence	12	8	17	11	6	17	16
Decreased motivation to study	6	4	9	3	5	6	14
Current living arrangement:							
Interracial dormitory	48	49	46	53	47	42	53
All-black or minority dormitory, floor, wing	4	3	5	2	4	4	7
Private off-campus apartment or rooming house	24	30	15	26	25	22	19
Parents' home	18	14	24	11	17	26	18
Preferred living arrangement:							
Interracial dormitory	20	17	24	23	18	18	21
All-black or minority dormitory, floor, wing	15	15	15	14	15	16	15
Private off-campus apartment or rooming house	46	50	42	49	48	44	47
Parents' home	9	6	12	6	9	10	9
Influence of race on choice of friends and activities:							
Dominant influence	41	41	43	49	41	37	42
Significant influence	27	29	24	18	29	32	25
Little influence	31	30	33	33	29	31	32
Ability of organized black students to influence programs:							
Yes, they're able to	57	58	56	58	61	55	53
Probably could, but haven't so far	24	21	27	23	21	27	24
No, they're unable to	19	20	18	19	17	19	23

(continued)

	Nat'l. Norm	Sex		Family Income			
		Male	Female	0-4,999	5,000-9,999	10,000-14,999	15,000+
Overall reaction to this college:							
Very satisfied	8	7	9	7	9	10	4
Somewhat satisfied	56	59	52	49	59	55	59
Dissatisfied	36	33	39	43	32	36	36
Negative characteristics of this college:							
Low percentage black enrollment	60	62	58	63	61	64	50
Low black faculty and administrative presence	60	58	63	59	58	62	63
Low accessibility of faculty and administrators	42	43	40	40	39	49	38
Lack of overt attempts to respond to blacks' needs	61	59	63	59	60	63	63
Victim of any aspect of racial discrimination here:							
Yes/Probably	49	51	46	49	43	49	55
No	51	49	54	50	57	51	45
Recipient of special favorable treatment because of race:							
Yes/Probably	27	26	29	25	29	24	31
No	73	74	71	75	71	76	69
If yes, reaction to special treatment:							
Positive	34	37	31	35	40	26	32
Negative	28	28	28	28	26	29	30
Ambivalent	14	13	15	8	14	18	13
Little or no reaction	12	15	8	7	11	17	11
College cares about having black students:							
Yes	18	18	18	25	15	20	15
No	67	67	66	62	67	68	69
Not sure	14	14	15	13	17	12	14
Changes which should be made for black students:							
More recruitment of black students and faculty	59	61	57	64	63	60	47
Revised admissions standards	4	4	3	5	2	4	4
More financial aid (especially for blacks)	41	40	42	35	43	43	43
Greater role for blacks in decision making	4	4	4	6	3	6	5
More remedial programs and tutoring	24	24	25	22	24	31	18
Curriculum changes to reflect relevance	5	5	6	4	6	5	5
Expansion of Black Studies	33	32	34	48	33	30	23
Purge of racists from staff	15	18	11	14	10	20	15
All-black housing	1	1	1	1	1	1	—
Black lounge or Center	1	1	1	1	1	2	1
More black activities, social life, cultural events	14	12	18	12	16	15	12
COLLEGE DEMOGRAPHIC DATA							
Region:							
Northeast	27	26	29	18	29	33	23
Midwest	36	39	32	32	35	33	47
South	24	24	25	34	26	19	18
West	13	12	15	16	11	15	12
Sponsorship:							
Public	67	65	68	62	68	72	65
Private	33	35	32	38	32	28	35
Size:							
Small	35	36	34	32	34	36	35
Medium	23	23	22	19	25	23	23
Large	42	41	44	49	41	41	42
Percentage black enrollment:							
Low	16	16	16	19	19	10	11
Medium	30	30	30	40	27	27	30
High	54	54	55	41	54	63	58
Location:							
Central City	41	44	38	46	45	31	44
Other Urban	45	41	49	38	43	53	44
Non-metropolitan	14	15	13	16	12	15	12

	Nat'l. Norm	College Year				College Generation	
		1st	2nd	3rd	4th	1st	Other
Age:							
17-18 years	23	62	16	5	2	17	26
19-20 years	41	30	63	50	18	34	45
21-22 years	21	3	11	30	44	25	18
23-26 years	12	4	7	12	27	17	9
27-35 years	3	—	2	3	8	7	1
Sex:							
Male	56	45	57	60	64	62	53
Female	44	55	43	40	35	38	47
Between the ages of 5 and 15, lived predominantly in a:							
Large city	56	54	61	55	55	52	59
Small city	23	20	19	26	28	24	22
Suburban area	10	13	11	8	7	10	10
Rural area	8	12	7	5	6	10	6
Home was located in:							
Same area as secondary school	89	88	94	79	94	90	88
Different area from secondary school	7	8	4	13	4	7	7
Secondary school was located in:							
Same area as college	78	77	79	81	76	77	78
Different area from college	20	22	21	14	21	22	18
Previously attended another college:							
Yes	25	10	21	28	44	29	23
No	69	83	73	66	49	64	72
If yes, it was a:							
Two-year public college	49	29	50	56	50	52	47
Two-year private college	6	16	3	3	7	3	8
Black college	10	27	7	14	6	8	12
Four-year, white, public college	26	20	30	19	30	32	22
Four-year, white, private college	13	—	12	11	19	16	11
Parents who attended college:							
Both	16	21	16	13	12	—	24
Father only	10	9	12	11	9	—	16
Mother only	15	18	15	11	15	—	23
Neither	59	52	57	64	65	100	37
Older brother(s) or sister(s) attended college:							
Yes	45	53	45	45	33	—	68
No	30	23	29	32	38	67	10
No; have no older brother or sister	25	24	26	22	29	33	21
Range of family's current annual income:							
Less than $5,000	18	19	15	21	18	24	16
$ 5,000-9,999	36	24	40	42	37	45	30
$10,000-14,999	25	30	26	22	24	21	28
$15,000-24,999	13	14	14	7	14	6	16
$25,000 and over	6	10	2	6	5	2	8
Major field of study:							
Social Sciences	17	16	11	23	21	18	17
Political Science and History	11	7	8	15	14	12	10
Business	15	15	15	9	19	14	15
Education	15	9	21	13	19	16	15
Biological Sciences	6	6	6	4	6	5	6
Engineering and Math	4	2	6	3	2	3	4
Physical Sciences	2	2	2	2	1	1	2
Health Professions (non-M.D.)	3	5	2	3	2	5	2
English	4	5	3	4	3	2	5
Fine Arts	4	4	6	4	4	5	4
Black Studies	1	—	1	—	2	2	—
Academic average:							
A	1	—	—	—	3	—	1
B	25	20	26	24	32	25	25
C	59	49	60	68	62	59	59
D or F	7	6	12	5	3	10	5

(continued)

	Nat'l. Norm	College Year				College Generation	
		1st	2nd	3rd	4th	1st	Other
Plans after graduation from college:							
Graduate school	45	39	39	54	51	42	46
Work	34	43	37	25	30	35	34
Work and Graduate school	10	7	10	10	14	12	9
Main source of money used to go to college:							
Family	20	24	24	15	16	7	27
Scholarship from college	29	36	29	23	25	31	27
Scholarship from other source	16	11	17	17	20	21	14
Loan from college	11	11	9	15	9	14	9
Loan from bank or credit union	6	6	4	8	7	5	7
Loan from other source	3	3	5	3	2	3	4
Personal savings	4	3	3	4	4	6	3
Wages from jobs held during college	6	1	5	7	10	7	5
Veterans' benefits	3	1	2	5	3	4	2
Rating of academic preparation:							
Excellent	10	12	9	10	10	12	9
Good	38	41	34	44	34	33	41
Fair	29	34	28	24	30	29	29
Poor	23	13	29	22	26	27	20
Characteristics important in selecting this college:							
General reputation or academic standing	48	52	52	47	40	42	52
Curriculum or faculty in one field or department	26	26	29	25	24	23	28
Scholarships or other financial assistance	53	59	50	54	49	61	49
Proximity to home	50	46	55	43	55	46	52
Large black population	6	5	10	2	5	6	6
Low cost	20	15	23	22	19	19	20
Size of student body	14	15	15	12	11	13	14
Knew others who were enrolled here	27	28	27	26	27	26	28
Admitted under special circumstances based on race:							
Yes/Probably/Perhaps	50	44	50	54	54	53	49
No	50	56	50	46	46	47	51
If yes, major effects on life here:							
None so far	59	67	56	64	50	53	63
Feel like an outsider: isolated, alienated	16	11	17	16	21	18	15
Pushed toward certain major or career	4	2	7	3	2	7	2
Resented by whites: idea that blacks get too much	9	8	8	9	9	8	9
Unchallenged; expected to be dumb, etc.	9	5	12	8	9	11	7
Estimated black attrition rate:							
0-10 percent	41	52	42	35	34	38	43
10-25 percent	15	10	19	14	18	18	14
25-50 percent	14	5	14	19	22	15	14
50 percent or over	9	5	7	14	13	10	9
Unknown	16	23	15	17	10	16	16
Most common reasons for black attrition:							
Academic reasons: pressure, poor preparation, etc.	63	51	67	69	66	67	61
Financial reasons	50	41	48	53	58	48	50
Black-white friction, racism, etc.	24	28	24	20	22	23	24
Frustration, confusion, isolation, etc.	38	33	37	43	41	37	38
Concerned about ability to meet college costs:							
Yes	47	48	53	46	39	48	47
No	53	52	47	54	61	52	53
If yes, concerned about:							
Cutbacks in special programs for blacks/minorities	31	29	27	35	34	35	28
Smaller amount of aid available each year	40	28	39	41	60	41	40
Amount of aid tied to maintaining high grade average	12	13	20	8	2	16	10
Insufficient money for personal expenses	17	17	20	17	15	14	20
If no, unconcerned because of:							
Adequate family resources	33	42	44	20	26	19	41
Four-year scholarship	40	44	29	45	41	47	36
Good job(s)	11	3	14	13	14	15	9
Adequate financial aid	25	25	24	27	23	24	25
Activities participated in:							
Black organizations on campus	47	41	50	41	59	48	47
Student government, college committees, etc.	11	6	15	9	15	11	11
Athletics	30	30	33	29	27	26	33
Radio station, newspaper, etc.	4	2	2	7	5	4	4
Club, choir, etc.	21	17	20	24	26	20	22
Tutoring, advising	7	3	7	5	16	8	7
Political activities off campus	5	1	5	3	13	6	5

	Nat'l. Norm	College Year				College Generation	
		1st	2nd	3rd	4th	1st	Other
Service activities off campus	10	2	8	8	24	11	9
None	25	29	27	26	18	24	26
Type of contact with faculty members outside class:							
Classwork-related only	36	42	35	34	30	36	36
Extra projects or reading	17	7	19	17	26	19	16
General academic subjects	20	15	19	25	22	21	20
Job/career prospects	14	10	12	13	21	14	13
Social	16	10	16	19	20	14	17
More with black faculty/Little with white faculty	22	16	22	23	29	25	20
Little or none	40	44	42	41	31	40	40
Special academic help received:							
Yes	34	32	38	36	29	37	33
No	66	68	62	64	70	63	67
If yes, evaluation of help received:							
Insufficient	23	17	15	27	38	27	21
Adequate	76	83	84	73	59	72	79
Too much: required remediation not needed	1	—	—	—	3	2	—
If no, response to lack of help:							
Ambivalent: help wasn't needed	79	70	80	86	81	84	76
Negative: help was needed but unavailable.	17	25	15	12	14	10	20
Intense academic competition among students:							
Yes	59	52	64	66	56	58	60
No	36	42	28	32	42	37	35
Not sure	3	4	6	1	—	3	3
Effect on student personally:							
Some	62	66	55	64	65	65	61
None	35	33	40	35	32	32	37
Not sure	3	2	4	1	3	3	3
If some, resulted in:							
Increased motivation to study	46	43	47	52	43	56	41
Harder work to compete with whites	37	39	34	39	37	43	33
Undermined self-confidence	12	12	14	8	13	11	12
Decreased motivation to study	6	4	5	8	7	2	9
Current living arrangement:							
Interracial dormitory	48	68	47	42	29	41	51
All-black or minority dormitory, floor, wing	4	1	6	6	5	4	4
Private off-campus apartment or rooming house	24	10	23	27	38	26	22
Parents' home	18	18	19	19	17	19	18
Preferred living arrangement:							
Interracial dormitory	20	36	17	13	11	17	21
All-black or minority dormitory, floor, wing	15	24	14	14	6	14	16
Private off-campus apartment or rooming house	46	31	46	53	60	46	47
Parents' home	9	5	13	10	8	6	10
Influence of race on choice of friends and activities:							
Dominant influence	41	40	44	41	40	36	44
Significant influence	27	25	29	26	29	32	25
Little influence	31	34	27	33	30	32	31
Ability of organized black students to influence programs:							
Yes, they're able to	57	52	60	63	54	53	60
Probably could, but haven't so far	24	30	20	20	24	25	23
No, they're unable to	19	17	20	18	21	23	17
Overall reaction to this college:							
Very satisfied	8	10	8	7	6	8	8
Somewhat satisfied	56	66	56	52	48	56	56
Dissatisfied	36	23	36	40	45	35	36
Negative characteristics of this college:							
Low percentage black enrollment	60	63	60	60	58	64	58
Low black faculty and administrative presence	60	63	53	61	65	60	60
Low accessibility of faculty and administrators	42	37	40	41	49	37	44
Lack of overt attempts to respond to blacks' needs	61	62	57	62	66	58	63

(continued)

(continued)

	Nat'l.	College Year				College Generation	
	Norm	1st	2nd	3rd	4th	1st	Other
Victim of any aspect of racial discrimination here:							
Yes/Probably	49	36	46	51	64	41	53
No	51	64	544	49	36	59	47
Recipient of special favorable treatment because of race:							
Yes/Probably	27	22	27	29	32	24	29
No	73	78	73	70	68	76	71
If yes, reaction to special treatment:							
Positive	34	41	38	25	34	41	32
Negative	28	31	30	33	20	34	25
Ambivalent	14	7	11	10	25	11	15
Little or no reaction	12	11	8	19	10	11	12
College cares about having black students:							
Yes	18	24	16	17	16	15	20
No	67	56	68	73	72	66	67
Not sure	14	19	16	10	11	19	12
Changes which should be made for black students:							
More recruitment of black students and faculty	59	51	60	63	64	58	60
Revised admissions standards	4	1	3	4	8	5	3
More financial aid (especially for blacks)	41	37	45	43	38	37	43
Greater role for blacks in decision making	4	2	5	3	8	4	5
More remedial programs and tutoring	24	25	20	30	22	24	24
Curriculum changes to reflect relevance	5	4	4	6	8	6	5
Expansion of Black Studies	33	30	27	35	41	36	31
Purge of racists from staff	15	10	17	16	18	9	18
All-black housing	1	—	—	2	1	1	1
Black lounge or Center	1	—	1	3	1	2	1
More black activities, social life, cultural events	14	12	16	14	15	11	16
COLLEGE DEMOGRAPHIC DATA							
Region:							
Northeast	27	21	27	30	31	33	24
Midwest	36	41	36	34	29	35	36
South	24	28	24	21	22	21	26
West	13	9	13	15	18	11	14
Sponsorship:							
Public	67	63	64	74	67	67	67
Private	33	37	36	26	33	33	33
Size:							
Small	35	39	39	26	36	38	34
Medium	23	19	21	27	25	20	24
Large	42	42	41	47	39	42	42
Percentage black enrollment:							
Low	16	19	16	14	14	17	15
Medium	30	32	29	29	30	29	31
High	54	49	55	57	56	54	54
Location:							
Central City	41	38	49	38	38	39	43
Other Urban	45	44	39	52	45	48	43
Non-metropolitan	14	18	12	10	16	13	14

WILLIAM BOYD II was Executive Director of the Educational Policy Center, Inc. when this study was conducted. EPC is a non-profit organization which stimulates equal opportunity in higher education through research and technical assistance. He also was a faculty member at Queens College of the City University of New York. EPC has emerged with A Better Chance, Inc. (ABC), a non-profit organization offering quality college preparatory education to economically disadvantaged young people, and Dr. Boyd has been named President of the combined ABC organization.

Dr. Boyd's activities include service on the Boards of Trustees of Deerfield Academy, The New York Public Library, Williams College, and the Whitney Young Memorial Foundation, as well as membership on the Advisory Committee for the American Council on Education's Cooperative Institutional Research Program. His published writings include articles in Change magazine and the College Board Review.

Dr. Boyd was born in Tuskegee, Alabama, raised in Atlanta, Georgia, and became the first black student to attend Deerfield Academy (Deerfield, Massachusetts). His educational accomplishments include a B.A. in Political Science from Williams College and an M.A. and Ph.D. in Political Science from the University of California, Berkeley.

BLACK STUDENTS AT WHITE COLLEGES
Charles V. Willie and
Arline Sakuma McCord

BLACK TEACHERS IN URBAN SCHOOLS:
The Case of Washington, D. C.
Catherine Bodard Silver

BUSING: THE POLITICAL AND JUDICIAL PROCESS
James Bolner and
Robert Shanley

DESEGREGATION AND CAREER GOALS:
Children of Air Force Families
Alice Yohalem with
Quentin B. Ridgley
Foreword by Eli Ginzberg

EVALUATING SCHOOL BUSING: Case Study of
Boston's Operation Exodus
James E. Teele

RACE MIXING IN THE PUBLIC SCHOOLS
Charles V. Willie with
Jerome Beker